DEAR FOLKS

DEAR FOLKS

A Soldier's Letters Home
1941 to 1961

Carol E. Yorke

Strategic Book Publishing and Rights Co.

Strategic Book Publishing & Rights Co., LLC
USA | Singapore
www.sbpra.net

For information about special discounts for bulk purchases, please contact Strategic Book Publishing and Rights Co. Special Sales, at bookorder@sbpra.net.

ISBN: 978-1-68181-285-4

ACKNOWLEDGEMENTS

Like any major project, *Dear Folks* owes its existence to a village of contributors. Most important was my part-time caregiver, Candi Camarillo, who gave her all-embracing support and encouragement on this year-long project, opening every envelope, organizing and maintaining the letters in chronological order, and then reading them out loud while I typed with my one functioning hand. This book would not have been possible without her.

A big thank you as well to three friends: Denette Huff, Bill Forman, and Ron Thomas for giving me their precious time and doing their best to decipher the virtually illegible handwriting of one or more letters when Candi was not available.

Thank you as well to several Fiverr freelance contributors:

Scott T. Martinez, editor
Daniel J. Eyenegho, cover designer
Russell Burgess, author bio
Shama Arige, book description

Table of Contents

Chapter One

On the Precipice of War

It was a chilling time: Only twenty-one years after the end of World War I—the Great War, or the war to end all wars—Germany again threatened the security of Europe by invading Poland on September 1, 1939. Two short days later, both France and Britain declared war. In a radio broadcast that day, British Prime Minister Neville Chamberlain briefly announced, ". . . [England] is at war with Germany." In an isolationist spirit during the 1930s, the Americans were loath to become embroiled in another foreign conflagration, and the Congress passed a series of laws, the Neutrality Acts, to ensure America in fact remained neutral.

Whereas his military advisors and Secretary of War counseled him to utilize America's extensive resources for its own domestic defense, President Franklin Delano Roosevelt was convinced that the defeat of the Nazis was more essential for US national security. Therefore, he promoted a plan to aid the cash-strapped allies without joining the war sweeping through Europe. Not to aid the Allies in their struggle against Germany, he believed, would be tantamount to helping their enemies.

The Lend Lease Act, approved by Congress in March 1941, skirted the neutrality provisions by giving President Roosevelt virtually unlimited authority to direct material aid—

ammunition, tanks, airplanes, trucks, and foodstuffs—when he deemed it necessary for US national security, without payment in return. Critics suspected that this law would be Roosevelt's means for ever so slowly sliding into war.

Scores of American young men, eager to jump into the fray, circumvented the American neutrality laws and joined either the British or Canadian Royal Air Force, while others stayed at home and joined the American military (oftentimes involuntarily by the draft instituted just the year before), just in case the US did eventually enter the European war.

However, it wasn't until after the Japanese attack on Pearl Harbor on December 7, 1941, that the United States did eventually respond with a declaration of war, first on Japan and then on Germany. Just over sixteen million Americans ultimately served during the Second World War, and the total number of US military deaths in battle and from other causes amounted to 407,316—a great price to pay.

Chapter Two

Leaving Home

Hal was doing his best to not notice the tears pooling in his mother's soft blue eyes. He knew exactly how she was feeling about the upcoming separation, because he felt the same, but his own sorrow was tempered by his anticipation for the new life opening before him.

It was a bleak, cheerless Oklahoma day in mid-May 1941, when Harold (Hal), a tall, lanky twenty-four-year-old man, his mother, Stella, and his best buddy, Borden, stood on the front porch of their home saying their last goodbyes. The boys were dressed in their most comfortable hitchhiking clothes—loose pants and shirts. Plus, they had decided to forego wearing hats. Stella had artfully pulled up her long, light-brown hair in a proper bun that morning just for this sad occasion and wore her favorite flowered dress with matching hat and shoes.

Stella and Hal's father had reluctantly accepted Hal's decision to join the Army; even so, she hoped and prayed that he would change his mind or that the Army would not accept him with his one blind eye when he got there. Hal waved the thought away when she mentioned this possibility and he had insisted on accompanying his friend anyway. "Just in case," he'd said. "Maybe, just maybe the Army will take me."

The last hugs were hugged and kisses kissed, and then the boys were off. "Be sure to write soon—and often. I love you, son, and will miss you terribly." Stella waved them off with the soft, pink-fringed white handkerchief that she had clutched tightly in her hand.

"I will. I love you too," he tossed back. "Say bye to Dad and Doris again, and give them kisses for me."

With that said, the two young men bounced down the steps and strolled down the street on their new adventure, whistling a cheery tune and turning to wave goodbye now and then as they ambled along. Stella watched them go through moist, unhappy eyes.

Since dawn, the angry black clouds hovering overhead had threatened rain, and soon they began a light sprinkle that washed away the warm, salty tears that Stella just realized were spilling down her drawn, crumpled face.

"Please, Lord, keep them safe and protect them on their long journey," she prayed.

As she watched the two boys striding down the city street heading north toward the highway, she thought how decidedly handsome they both were: Hal, slim, six feet five inches tall, with coal-black hair, a strikingly pale moustache, tanned complexion, and intelligent, blue eyes that spoke volumes. "Clark Gable handsome," people said. Borden was apparently the same height, she noticed, but he had more meat on his bones and lighter hair and complexion.

"Watch out world, here they come," she said with a smile as she turned back into the small brick house to start her morning chores.

Rather than starting her work, however, Stella melted onto the pillowed living room sofa, recalling the day when they had first realized that Hal couldn't see out of his right eye.

"Hey, Mom, Bobby can see out of both eyes," twelve-year-old Hal announced as he sat down at the kitchen table for the noon meal one warm spring Oklahoma day.

"Yes, of course," she responded.

Sitting back in the ladder-back chair and breathing in the warm, delicious smells of the pot roast simmering on the stove, he wondered aloud, "You can too," he blurted. "I can't!"

"You can't?" she gasped. "Nothing?"

"No, I only see fuzzy forms with my right eye."

"My word," she protested, "why didn't you tell us this before? How long has your sight been so bad?"

"I don't know. I never thought anything about it. I just figured that everybody sees like I do. I don't ever remember being able to see anything differently."

"Wow," he enthused, "imagine that—two eyes. That'd be swell, like a cowboy with two guns or a kid with two slingshots!"

"You poor thing!" She gently pulled him into her arms and hugged him tightly. "I never imagined that you couldn't see very well. You do everything that any other boy can do, you are a champ at tennis, and you don't seem to have any problems in school."

"Now, now," he comforted, "it's no sweat."

Soon, she found herself sobbing there on the living room sofa, her thoughts bouncing back and forth from that day to this.

When Stella saw Hal next, he had regaled her, his dad, and sister, Doris, with the story of how he had passed the eye test to get into the Army:

"The doctor told me to cover one eye and read the chart, so I covered my blind, right eye with my right hand. No sweat, I read the chart just fine, of course. Then the doc asked me to cover the other eye and read the chart, so I lowered my right hand and replaced it with my left to cover the same eye. No sweat, I read the chart without a hitch.

"'You passed,' the doctor told me.

"'I did?' I said.
"'Yep,' he said, and just like that I was in the Army."

Over the next twenty years, the length of his service in the Army, Hal wrote to his folks (his dad, mom, and sister Doris) when he could, albeit sporadically—occasionally with gaps of weeks, months, and for a long stretch, even years. Stella hoarded his treasured letters protectively in an airtight, tin, blue container under her bed. After Stella died in 1963, Hal's wife, Wilda, removed the letters from the tin container and stuffed them into an outstretched shoebox tucked in her closet.

In 2006, when Wilda, my mother, passed away, I appropriated the letters to compile them into this book. I remembered clearly how much I had enjoyed dad's letters from Korea when I was a teenager, and I had long wanted to compile them into a book for others to enjoy and to experience the essence of an ordinary (though extraordinary to me) soldier's life during two decades of Army life, beginning June 1941, more than six months before the Japanese surprise attack on Pearl Harbor and before the United States's entry into World War II, continuing until he retired from the Army in 1961.

It may be hard now in the twenty-first century to recall or even imagine the days before computers, emails, texts, and tweets, but the truth is that once upon a time, before these modern wonders, families and friends communicated with each other through handwritten or typed letters and postcards—"snail mail," as it is now called. Imagine sending a letter to a loved one and having to wait weeks or even months to receive a reply. That is virtually incomprehensible for those of us used to almost instantaneous responses to our messages.

Yes, people used telephones; however, they leave no history, no permanent record.

I have transcribed Hal's letters from his originals, exactly as he wrote them, without editing. In this way, it is as if you were reading his original letters. If you are obsessed with good English, as I am, you might cringe as you read along, but I hope you can ignore the errors and enjoy the essence of the story he relates.

Chapter Three

In the Army Now

Postmark: June 21, 1941

Sat. 20th

Dear Folks:

Don't let the pictures fool you—this is like any other business—no snap.

However, this is the first time I've been in such close association with men. For the most part, the fellows are ok. Of course, there are some chickens—you find them anywhere. The Army is ok as far as I am concerned. We are about 1 mile from the Miss R. Here it isn't so big tho. It only looks deep and muddy—flowing slowly by. Haven't been here long— got in last Thurs. about 11:00. Am still tired from so much traveling. The food here isn't as good as that at Tacoma (Ft. Lewis).

Well, I've been in the army for over a week now and I have yet to hear a Bugle. The S. Sgt. wakes me up with his big loud voice. Mealtime is done the same way—Must close and get to bed—lites out at 9:00.

Azever with love,
Hal

P.S. I'll probably be here for about 4 months. If you all should happen to write sometime, just address me at the Reception Center, Jefferson Barracks, Mo.

* * *

Dear Mom:

Well, yesterday I saw St Louis—all of it I ever want to see. From now on I'll do my sightseeing on the post. If I had a car I'd have enjoyed the visit, but just to walk around and try to see a city so large is foolish, to say the least. My pass was good until 11:00 Sun morn. I came in about 11:00 last nite. If I go to school and get an AM rating, and later a corporal's rating ($40 per month) I automatically lose the rating and pay (AM rating $70). I'd go to $70 when I got the AM, then back to $40 when and if I got Corp. stripes. If I stayed here and got my stripes, then went to school and got a rating, I'd get $80. I have a good chance to get them.

* * * *

Postmark: August 13, 1941

Thursday

Dear Dad:

Surely, I was glad to hear from you. I was certain that you'd come out all right on probation. I'm sure that you'll get along fine from now on, too.

Well, everything is rosy for me too. I've tried to get a 10 day furlough, but every time I mention it I get a baleful fish stare from the Sargt. Finally have given up the idea. Maybe I'll get a furlough at Xmas. Here's hoping.

Dad, this hospital stretch is due to my own foolishness. I am sure that my work at C. & C. is responsible. The doc told me that I had been doing too much heavy lifting—You know how I've always been. Try to show how much heavy lifting I can do. Then too, I haven't felt right since I had the flue—while going to school in Amarillo. One or the other, or both, fixed up my kidneys for me. They must be o.k. now, because I'm going back to duty. If I wasn't fit, they'd give me a M.D. [medical discharge]

I'm feeling fine & have been for quite a while. Of course, it limits me to look at the flabby muscles on arms, legs, & chest, but I'll harden up in a few months. But certainly, the whole thing is my fault & no one else's. I wasn't told to kill my fool self at C. & C. Anyway, guess it was just one of those things that happen. It's a good thing I could go to the hospital without worrying about the doc, nurses, medicine. Now that I'm out, I believe I am better off for my experience. Here's one little lad that will watch himself from now on.

I owe $5.82 on the suit, I'm sure. I made a $10 down payment and, about a week later, I paid the monthly payment—before I received the suit even. I made 3 other payments then. Just before I left Amarillo, I paid the last (paid Sat. nite & left Sunday). What would you do if you were me? I haven't written them yet. I haven't been able to do anything about it. I can't put money in the mail & can't get out to get a postal money order. Besides, I'll not pay more than I owe. Must close till later.

Love,
Hal

What's Dorothy's address?

* * *

Friday

Dear Mom:

On the suit, I paid \$10.down & \$7 the next time. The payment was due. I made payments on time including one the day before I left Amarillo. I should owe about \$12.82 instead of \$19.82. But I'm writing a card to explain that I'm in the army and will pay them as soon as possible, probably after Xmas—or would you?

Look for a college Physics by Foley. Keep it & sell the one by Kimball—you listed it in your letter.

The story I was referring to was the nightmare—or what have you—about what happened when I got out of the hospital. I don't want any of the themes, etc. now. But keep that stuff. Maybe when I'm an older man I'll dig it up & amuse myself with it.

You will have to mail the books at the P. office at "book rate." Don't let them tell you that you have to pay more than 3¢ for the biggest book (You were being robbed on the post, I believe—6¢ postage!). It may be cheaper to Xpress or send by freight. You will be lucky if you get \$2 out of the bunch. I have a price catalogue from the Col. Book Co. Send the books or write, but go ahead.

You say something about a note among my things saying I owed \$5.82 on the suit, if it's a receipt, o.k. If not, I was probably just figuring. Did you find any of the receipts? The last one? (dated about June 6—or the day we left Amarillo.)

If the book isn't listed in the catalogue the book co. won't buy the book unless it's a new issue—or new publication.

Did you find any pictures (snapshots)? Have you given away the old racket?

As I said before, I'm in no special hurry for the stuff. If you find College Algebra I'd like to have it too.

Are you getting all our books together? Are you adding some of the better fiction that was left in the basement by the former owners? Maybe someday will have a home with book cases 'n everything. We'll have a nice library if we ever do.

Remember, I'll be in this man's army for three years. Anything that you run into that you don't think I can use <u>now</u> or wasn't want when I get back home, throw out. At least heap it up in a pile, write & describe it, then I'll tell you if I'll want it. Perhaps you'd better make a photocopy of the above paragraph and file to settle future arguments.

Love to you & Doris. Keep the dust flying!!!

Azever with love,
Hal

Chapter Four

It's All About a Girl

Hal and Borden sauntered along a crowded street in downtown San Antonio one unusually warm August day. Hal was whistling as clear as a bell the tune of the popular Harry James song, "You Made Me Love You,"[1] while Borden concentrated on the view ahead.

A long-legged brunette in high-waist silky trousers that swayed with the swing of her slender hips walked half a block ahead of them; Borden was captivated, emitting a low whistle in appreciation.

"I know that gal," Hal boasted.

"You do not," Borden scoffed. "I'll bet you five bucks that she'll shut you down if you go flapping your lips at her."

"You're on—the easiest fiver I've ever made," Hal said with a laugh as they watched the beauty in question turn into the five-and-dime store at the corner.

Both young men increased their paces to catch up with her, with Hal reaching the door first and quickly stepping into the shop.

Borden followed and watched fascinated as Hal approached the girl browsing the greeting cards on a tall center rack. The dark-haired beauty glanced over to see this tall drink of water standing over her, her big dusky eyes rolling leisurely from the

---

[1]   https://www.youtube.com/watch?v=bMaCoxOGXPM&list=RDbMaCo xOGXP

tip of his tie up to his white-toothed grin. "Why, Hal Yorke!" she exclaimed, astonished, a cheerful smile blossoming on her lovely face. "I don't believe what my own eyes are seeing. What in the world are you doing here?"

"Oh, hi, Wilda," he replied nonchalantly. "Borden, my friend here, and I joined the army a couple months ago, and we're in town on leave for a few days. What are you doing in San Antonio?"

"Oh, I moved down here and got a cashier's job at the bank down the street a couple of years ago after I graduated from high school. I share a room with a friend in a boarding house not far from here."

"It's nice to see you again," Hal replied. "Wilda, do you remember Borden? He lived in Guymon, down the street from me. Borden, this is Wilda, the smartest gal in all of Oklahoma; she was only fifteen when she graduated high school."

Hal's two friends hadn't met before. However, Borden remembered her older brother, Earl, who worked at the gas station just outside of town. The three chatted for a while, exchanging stories about mutual friends and acquaintances. "Let me buy you a Coke at the lunch counter before you go," Hal invited.

"My, yes," she smiled, her eyes looking soulfully up at him, "I'd enjoy that. I don't have to be back at work for an hour, and that would give us more time to talk."

"Swell," Hal sputtered, delighted.

There was something appealing about Wilda that he had never noticed in their previous encounters at home, where she had been a much younger girl living on a farm just outside of Guymon, forever dressed in other girls' hand-me-down clothes. She was taller than most girls, five feet seven, he guessed, and her guileless bright eyes and sweet smile were so alluring.

Hal turned to walk to the low, black counter hugging the back wall, waving his arm for them to follow.

All seven stools lined along the counter were vacant, and Hal claimed the centermost one, indicating that the other two should sit on the stools on either side of his.

"You first, madam," he offered, watching as she delicately perched herself on the seat. Placing his forearms on the low counter for stability, Hal wrapped his long legs around the base of the stool as he essentially squatted until his seat settled on the stubby red-cushioned stool.

The three friends enjoyed their Cokes and stimulating conversation until it was time for Wilda to go back to work.

Hal was determined that he would see her again.

* * *

Postmark: September 13, 1941

Sun.

Dear Dad:

Well, I wrote a long letter to Mom about the past week's activities & asked that she send it to you. But I know how it is to get mail. You would probably like to hear from me directly, too.

I'm feeling fine—never better—and am ready for the army. I've taken all tests & wait now only for assignment for school. I took the I-test over again (they'd lost records from Seattle), and made a better grade than before—146. Last time I made 138—which was unusually high. I took three other tests & believe I passed all. For one—Metal Worker's Test—I may not have done so well. But I'm sure I passed. I made good on Mechanical measurements Test.

Also, my math test I did pretty well on. I'll never know just what I did make. Only if I don't pass, I'll hear about it.

They are asking for volunteers for Puerto Rico post. Of course, I watched the other fools sign up. Some of old timers say nothing there but Negroes, mosquitoes, and malaria which are not for me. I'll take north-west for mine. May sign up for Alaska after I get A.M. rating—about a year from now—I hope.

Also, they came in today asking for truck drivers. Yours truly has asked for that job for several reasons:

(1)   I won't have to march,
(2)   It's easy work compared to K.P. (Kitchen Police) and other details,
(3)   I'll get to see St Louis & the post without walking,
(4)   Time will pass faster with that type of job,
(5)   If they put me on permanent party (may even tho. I wanted to get to school right away. Could be sent to school later), I'll have a better chance for corp. rating—maybe even Sargt.

I met a kid from Guymon [Oklahoma] the other morning. Name??? Shattuck. He worked at Charlie Ford's station. He use to be a great big fat kid. He's lost 40 lbs. since then & I didn't recognize him at first. He said he wouldn't have known me if he hadn't heard the instructor call my name—my mustache is responsible. Oh, you should see it. When I get my camera— Mom is sending it my new address on it. But I never think until it's too late. I've sent my new address to Marches & they should send my coat soon. According to my last letter from them they were expecting Tacoma Marches during the latter part of last month.

These planes really make the noise. Begin about 5:30 in morn. & go all day & most of nite. Our barracks is about ½ block from the apron, where the ships are lined up after each flight. These are the secondary trainers—600 h.p., low wing, all metal, also have some twin motored light bombers used for navigation training. The lite bombers are almost as fast as the two-seated pursuit. Bombers have 2-450 h.p. engines. They are really dangerous ships—wing speed is no more than the 2 seaters. They have no soaring power at all—depend entirely on the motors. If the motor quits, the ship drops like a stone. The instructors take up the mechs. On his ship—when he has no student with him. I hope to take a trip down into Florida soon. Officers are really nice fellows here. Most of them are about my age.

Well, guess I'll close for now. I have another letter all written, ready to mail. I couldn't find it, so I had to write another.

Guess this is my permanent base. Dad, could you get to Pensacola, Fla. Of course it would be best to stay with those fellows there that know you. But if you can sensibly make the change, swell.

Love,
Hal

Doris: We have no P.X. here so can't get any more air corps. jewelry right away! But I'll keep looking.

Mom: What about the house in Guymon. How are you going to collect rent, care for repairs, etc.? Are the Macs using our furniture? if so, $25 isn't enuff.

Well, we mechanics must keep up our vitality if we're going to keep 'em flying.

Chow call is sounding.

* * *

Postmark: October 13, 1941

Saturday

Dear Mom:

Well, at last I can write from the barracks and not the hospital. I got out this morning. My disposition went thru without a hitch. I should leave here within a month and go to school at Chanutte Field (With Borden). Right now my main worry is to stay out of the hospital. I don't think that I could stand another hitch. When I left I was one of the oldest patients in the ward. I'll write when I get straightened out. I have to locate my bag of clothes and more important, my flight. I am writing this before I even get my uniform.

Love,

Hal

I have today and tomorrow to get ready for duty. Write me at my flight from now on.

Sat. Com officer got me a pass, I'll go into St Louis to show. Letter follows.

* * * *

Postmark: September 13, 1941

Flight 13, 355th School Squadron, Saturday morning

Dear Dad:

Well, I get out this morning. As soon as the clothes room opens I'll get my uniform and go merrily on my way. Today I have to locate my flight and my bag of clothes. Tomorrow I can lay around and rest—I hope. Within a month I should be on my way to Chanutte Field, Ill.—with Borden.

In the meantime I'll dodge all doctors and physical inspection. I'll be leary of them for the rest of my army life. I'll write a letter as soon as I know anything for sure, worth writing.

Write me at my flight from now on.

Love,
Hal

Sat.

Com. Officer got me a pass. I'll go to St Louis this aft. & go to shows, see town.

* * * *

Postmark: October 13, 1941

Oct. 13, 1941

Dear Folks:

Well, I'm at a really fine field now. The food is good, the officers treat us like white men. In the north they make no distinction between white & black. Here a white man is treated like one.

The commanding officer at J.B. is just another Grady T.

Jack Shattuck was sent to Las Vegas, Nev. a few days before I left J.B. He thought he was getting a nice place. He didn't like it there.

This town of Albany is about 20,000, very quiet, but has gambling & selling of mixed drinks, out in the open. But a funny thing the soldiers here are gentlemen. At J.B. they were like a lot of animals. The people here are friendly. The post has about two thousand soldiers.

Sat. morning, a Lieut. asked for former auto & airplane mechanics to step forward. I was among those who took the fatal step. Now I'm on the "line" at night. Each of us is assigned to a group which has a plane of its own to care for. I work from 3:00 in the aft. Till ???? in the morning. This goes on for 2 wks. then I'm on day shift for 2 wks.

I'm in Flt. A, 95th SS. The Flt. doesn't need to be on the envelope—This is a small field—95th SS., Turner Field, Ga. is enuf.

Well, I'm about 3,000 mi. from you now. The only thing that keeps me from signing up for Foreign Service & receiving double pay is that they no longer pay double for that. So yours truly will stay in the U.S. until requested to leave.

Next mo. I'm due to receive $30 pay, an $9 raise in 4 mos. That's better than I did at C. & C. That hospitalization is what I appreciate from the army. If you think that 84 days wasn't a hell, you just think again, but still I was glad to get it.

I've got some pictures of Georgia peaches. Really beautiful. This state raises a lot of 'em. It's called the peach state. One picture I like particularly—a blank. This is beautiful down here. They have green trees—in fact the town & country around here is just like Cuero [Texas].

My buddy & I (Bob Jones, 6", 180#) are planning a trip to Jacksonville Fla., about a couple wks. from now. It's a 195 mi. trip, but soldiers in uniform have no trouble getting rides. I can add another state to my collection.

If I had thot I could have gotten my change of address to you on the same day I left J.B. for 25¢. I could have sent you one of those birthdays greeting specials with.

* * *

Postmark: November 13, 1941, Albany, GA

Nov. 8. 1941

Dear Folks:

It seems that I'm having a little trouble finding enuff time to do anything at all. I'm still working nites—and days.

We moved from one barracks to another the other day. When we have nothing to do but sleep, we wash windows or clean up around the building.

For Thanksgiving we get about 4 or 5 days off, don't know which. I'm thinking about going to Cuero [Hal's hometown in South Texas]—if they'll feed me a turkey dinner. May try to take a nice fellow I know here along—if Grandma sez o.k. (or Mabel, or somebody). Xmas we get 10 days off. I may be able to stretch a point (not take Thanksgiving leave) and get 15 or 20 days for Xmas besides the 2 are too close together as far as paydays are concerned.

Got a letter from Sue Walker the other day. She's attending Univ. of Tex. majoring in accounting. Phil is there at Austin attending police officers training school. He will be a state patrol man when he finishes.

Borden graduates soon—don't know when—from mech. school at Chanutte. Mr. M is very ill. I don't expect he will last much longer. He was operated on for kidney stones. Now he's down with pneumonia (?). Borden is on his toes—needs to leave at a moment's notice, hoping he can finish school before the call comes.

We have just received another shipment of English Cadets to train to fly. Most of the guys here—officers included—don't think they're worth a ----- as fliers. They surely know how to wreck a plane without crashing, I'll say that for them. But then, all beginners are bad, I guess. I've tried to run on to some from The Pit, near Ely, Islehaus. Their accent is like the guys from around Boston. Not the cockney English. So far, I haven't had much luck finding one from near Dorothy.

Well, I now have 5:15 in the air. One hr. was nite flying in an AT-6A.

Two hours & 15 minutes was in an AT-7A (twin motored job). I think I'll solo soon.

Finally got hot water into our barracks. We're really enjoying the unusual. Also, we have some lite bulbs issued & can now write or read after dark. Also have heat in barracks now.

Armistase day some of the fellows had to "stand to" for a parade in town. My O.D. (wool) soon—I'll send a picture.

At the U.S.O. (by the way, we soldiers <u>have</u> to pay to that, too) they have enlarger & dark room where we can develop our pictures.

I'm getting lined up pretty well now & getting to where I want to take off week-ends & wear civilian clothes. I'm trying to get Mom to send my trunk with my new brown suit & other clothes, but realize she's awfully busy, so won't be disappointed if she can't do it. She probably has the trunk packed full of things & would have to empty it, then find a place for the stuff taken out.

Maybe next time I write I'll have my fountain pen. Mom is sending it with a lot of other junk.

My address—if I haven't given it before—
Pvt. HW Yorke
Flt. 13, 355 S.S.
Jefferson Barracks, Mo.

It's almost chow time. At supper we have to wear Class A. uniform—cotton kakhis (?), shoes shined, buttons buttoned, etc. Everything just right. Our flight has the reputation of being neatest on the post—a swell outfit. Our commander, Lt. Wire is really a swell chap. Very considerate of us rookies.

Well, write when you have time. Take care of yourself in that cold, damp climate out there.

How's the car. Wat do you do with yourself over the week-ends? Why don't you get a cheap set of clubs—or borrow some—& get out & play a little golf. Bet they have some real water hazards. Remember this is your time to enjoy your work.

If the week-ends seem long, just take up the old golf game again. It really would shorten the days.

Azever with love,

Hal

* * *

Dear Mom,

Well, I've seen about a week of real Army life and like it fine. The past week I've been getting all my tests. I had to take them all because records from Wash were lost. But then I made, walk around. Last time I made 138 and 2 test this time I got 146—which is above average. I took a math test mech. movements test—also a metal worker's test. I'm sure I did fine on the first two. The last—I dunno. Our new mess hall has been opened and don't have so far to walk.

Each day I get up at 5:30 (make beds and begin to clean up barracks). At 6:15 we line up and march about ¼ mi. to chow. At 8:00 we are back at barracks cleaning up. About 8:30 we fall in to and drill till about 11:00. At 11:30 we leave for chow again. At 1:00 we fall in again and drill till about 3:30—then fall out to clean up and dress in class. A uniform (have been in blue denim fatigue clothes till then). At 4:30 we fall in for retreat, parade to parade grounds, march around field and return to chow—then to barracks. We're then off for the day—unless given special detail.

All soldiers on post are given class B pass (can leave after retreat, except Sat. when we can leave at 1:00 as we only stand retreat Mon, Tues., Wed., and Thurs. and don't have to be back until 1:00 in the morning). Nearly every nite something is going on—usually free (dance, musical recital, etc.). Once a week, we have to buy a ticket to some show here on the post—WPA or some such. This is the only thing I don't like. In the papers I've seen places where a soldier has about $2.00 per week to spend for amusement. How? Is what I like to find out as it sometimes takes 3 wks. to get clothes back, we wash everything except uniforms ourselves. Our sheets are issued clean once a week. This is not included.

* * *

Dear Folks:

I am appropriating some government property [typewriter] to write you a letter about the latest developments—also to get in some practice on this machine.

You are probably wondering what is going on—I haven't written for so long. Well, the truth of the matter is that I have been busy and, then too, I haven't had any stamps. I am so behind in my letter writing that I'll never catch up. You see, my records from J.B. were delayed so that I didn't get paid with the rest of the boys. All the borrowing I could do, I did to get money for tobacco.

Well, I worked on the line—playing nursemaid to a bunch of planes with my arms in grease up to my elbows, until I decided that I had all of that that I wanted. My break came unexpectedly.

I was working on K.P.

The Lt. made me K.P. "pusher." All I had to do was to see that the other fellows worked. I did, but I worked with them. Several of them remarked to me that it was the first time they had seen a pusher work. I would assign someone to a dirty job, and then I'd go there and work with him. Also I made the guys change jobs after every meal so that no one of them would get the snaps. Many's the time I've seen the friends of the chaser loaf around all day and some poor guy do the work. I worked the devil out of the boys. We finished earlier than any bunch had ever finished.

Anyway—one of the fellows on K.P. knew of a vacancy in the engineering supply doing office work, filing, typing, etc. He asked if I could type. You know what happened. I have the job with the Lt that signs all passes, furloughs, recommendations for ratings, etc. I'm right in the office so should be able to make impression and a rating. Nothing much has happened since I last wrote.

I have 7 ½ hours in the air now. I went up in an AT 7 the other day. We went up to 7,800 feet, which is darn high when you consider that this place is at sea level or thereabouts. So far I have more time in than any of the other boys from J.B. In addition to that, I have in one hour of night flying and I've ridden in both the AT6A and AT7A. 7A has two 450 h.p. low-wing, cabin job, put out by Beach Craft. 6A has one motor, 625-5 h.p. low-wing canopy covered, twin cockpit job.

Now I have a swivel chair job. All this furniture is new. This machine really must have taken a beating, because two of the keys are bent out of line, but I will fix that. I'll just bend them the other way. Incidentally, I type much faster than anyone else here. With a little practice I should get up even more speed. I haven't done any typing since I was at Norman, remember?

Hours at my new job aren't so good right now. But in a week or two I'll change hours with someone on the day shift. I work from 4:30 to????, usually about 12:30 so I guess I'll sign off and finish tomorrow. Don't get my money until then anyway.

I didn't get the money today so can expect a payday every day. The others may look forward to one day a month.

Love,
Hal

Xmas gift suggestions?

December 1, 1941

Am afraid I didn't get my 15-day furlough until after Xmas.

* * *

Postmark: Dec 11, 1941 Denver, CO

Guess you folks got my night letter. I didn't use train ticket but did my commanding officer send a telegram to me there? I had a 15 day furlough begin Dec. 8. I was going to surprise you, but got a surprise instead. Mr. M is getting along swell, should be working in a few mos. Letter when I and if I get to Ga.

Hal

* * * *

Postmark: December 13, 1941 Albany, GA.

We forget about the sweater for a while. I have so much on my mind just now. Honestly, I can't talk about it but I am busy and have so much to think about right now. Let me accustom myself to the new situation before you expect any measurements. Please I can't do it now! I appreciate it Mom and I want a sweater, but right now I can't write a few necessary letters and take care of all this other mess. Just accept a few things without asking why or trying to keep reminding about the sweater. I am sick and so disgusted right now.

Probably when I catch up on my sleep I'll feel better. I won't forget the measurements—just don't remind me again, pleez. I hope to get some pics made as soon as I get time, which may be too late for Xmas. Remember, we can't leave the post or a gosh-darn thing right now. What a mess! Maybe in about a year I'll get everything straightened out. I'll try to never write another letter like this one.

It's so foolish, childish, etc. I have to let it go this time. When you get my next letter you'll see the diff. I just need sleep right now.

Love, Hal

* * *

December 13, 1941

Dear Folks:

My action in reporting so promptly (Mon., 8:00) received favorable comment from my commanding officer, Capt. Reid. He complimented me before the engineering officer, Lt Frost, a Capt. Wiennieser, & my Sargt. Doughty. I was the first to report.

As I wrote, I didn't use the train ticket. I should scold you for buying it in the first place. But under the circumstances, both of us being so disappointed in the result of the furlough, I can't scold much.

Here is the whole story—Right after I told you that I would get 16 days, beginning Dec. 12, the order came out here at the field cancelling all furloughs. When I got the news concerning my ticket, I went to Capt. Reid & explained the situation. He gave me an emergency furlough. I thot it might be cancelled (at any time) so I hadn't let you know I was coming.

I used Amarillo as a resting place. I hadn't had any sleep at all when I got there. (Left here Fri. aft. 5:30 a.m., Amarillo 5:30 Sun morn.) I was going to leave there Mon. morn. After the news of all furloughs being cancelled I knew that I'd never be able to make it all the way to Calif. without being picked up.

Military police were meeting all buses & trains, & placing soldiers on the next returning train. I'd have only got there & had to leave without even seeing you. I'd have had the expense of a return ticket, too. Have you got your money back on the ticket yet? Left Amarillo Tues. 11:00 in the morning. I got a little vacation anyway. I'm so darn sore about all this mess up. Sometimes I think I'll find me some nice gal, earning her own living of course, and get married. But I'm afraid that would only make matters worse. I've got the nice girl—but can't see me asking her to give up that to become a soldier's wife. She'd have to live "way up yore" & me "way down bygone." You can see that I'm out of my head. Put it down to loss of sleep, please. If I don't mention it again, let's just forget about it. It's probably just a passing thot.

Any kind of box, at any time surely would be appreciated.

* * *

December 25, 1941

Dear Folks:

It looks like I'll just have to be content with being in the same country with you—which isn't a whole lot of comfort.

We worked all day Xmas—couldn't even leave the post. I had a good dinner. Menu is enclosed. Xmas eve I went into town (wasn't supposed to, but I just decided the whole Army wasn't going to keep me on the post Xmas day & eve, also). A friend & I met 2 gals & they took us to their home. Had a swell time, but couldn't accept their invite to dinner Xmas.

We are having all kinds of blackouts, drills, practice alarms, etc. This is in addition to regular duty. We don't mind it tho. Those things are necessary but this Xmas restriction. Thank God you aren't near here. You'd only hear us cuss about it. You should see my clothes line. I'm on the blacklist around here. My clothes show that "tattle-tale" gray. Sox & shorts are draped on a post at the head of my bed to a nail on a wall at my bed foot.

I've heard from grandma, Ethel Lee & Cloyd & Ethel. I didn't send a single Xmas card to anyone. I'm going to tell them all about getting into the hosp., but forget to say when I got out.

Enclosed is a pic I got when in Amarillo. I still haven't got the pics taken with my camera.

Well, I'll write again. Right now I ain't in the mood.

Love, Hal

Chapter Five

On the Home Front

Sunday Jan. 19, 1942

Dear Doris:

How are you? Do you get to see much scenery? Dad said that you all are taking some rides into the mountains. How do you like the west coast? It really makes Guymon look sick, doesn't it?

When I hitch-hiked to Amarillo, on my way to Calif., I almost stopped at Ft Worth to see Nellie Fisk, Dot, Dearleen, and Mr. Fisk. But it was about 7:00 in the evening, and I was afraid they would want me to stay over the night. If I had felt I could spend another night on the road, I'd never have left Amarillo when I did.

I don't remember if I told you or not, but in Amarillo, I went by Clove and Cowan's and saw three men in the warehouse I had worked with. One was the pump man that I made a few trips with installing those good Pomana Pumps, another fellow that was receiving clerk when I was there, and Mr. Mann, the warehouse foreman. The truck driver that almost took me to Calif. with him that xx time was there, too. All the other fellows had left. One went to the army—the others are at the shelter there in Amarillo. You should have seen the type of guys there now! I don't believe that the W.P.A. would have them as a gift!

Georgia is a beautiful state—from the ground. There are lots of pretty pine trees, gravel roads, and the old style of southern mansion. Few of the old homes are in bad state of repair. They keep these old places looking nice. I saw one place that the people told me about 80 years old. It was painted nicely and looked beautiful. Of course the grounds around it made the place look cramped—the house was built to preside over a huge plantation.

Two or three acres of terraced lawns are pretty, but still look small with such a large house in its center.

From the air, you see only patches of trees that look like scrub oak, barn-like houses, swamp, and water—mostly the last two. It really looks desolate. I wondered at first how anyone could make a living on such land. But the soil is fertile, and quite a number of people make comfortable incomes from a plot of ground, pitted with swampy places. They make more money from peanuts here than any other one thing.

I went thru a peanut factory at Dawson, Ga. a few weeks ago. It was a large place—mostly storerooms. The factory itself is like a large thrashing machine. The nuts are shelled by rollers, cleaned, culled by machinery. Women cull them by hand at the last. The peanuts come by them on endless belts, then are passed on to the storage bins. When we left there, the fellow gave each of us a big sack of nuts. We had gotten to know him fairly well by that time, so he took us home with him for supper. Later he wanted to take us back to Albany, but we refused, knowing that we could hitch-hike and make almost as good time—without the trouble to him. His wife really fed us a fine meal, steak, salad, French fries, dessert and honest to goodness civilian coffee. After the meal, she mentioned waffles, guess what! All three of us sat there and ate a meal of waffles. The sirup was homemade cane. (I tried to get them to let me use sorgum, but they had none fit for human consumption.)

31

Most of these soldiers, on payday, go into town and buy the biggest, thickest, juiciest steaks they can find. At camp we rarely get steaks, and when we do, they are so thin that you can see through them on a cloudy day. In fact, some of the pilots use our steaks to replace a broken eye piece in their goggles. A lucky man will get one thick enuf occasionally to use for shoe soles. Some of the more foolhardy, myself among this group, eat the things.

It really is amazing how well the men get along together. I don't believe it would be possible anywhere else but in the service. We rarely have any trouble, fights, or arguments that go beyond control. You see all kinds in this army. I met a young fellow the other day who had a Doctor's degree in English. (I believe Ethel spent the better part of her lifetime working on such a degree.) Then you run into a guy that hasn't enuf sense to pour water out of a boot, with directions written on the heel.

Well, I'll write again soon. You do the same.

Love,
Hal

* * *

Postmark: January 19, 1942

Dear Folks: (Darn that red ribbon!)

I am still hearing that that the men in this corps area will be given furloughs in the near future. But, as usual, I am not placing too much confidence in what I hear. You can rest assured that if I possibly can, I'll get one of those things and wend my merry way to you.

I wrote Mable, Grandma, and Bert. But so far, I've managed to mail only Mable's. I figured that she would need a cheering up much more than G. or B. I know just about what she'll go thru for the next couple of months! And it certainly isn't pleasant. You all write her just as often as possible. Describe the scenery, send pictures (not cards), and wise-crack. Try to space your letters so that two letters (one from Mom and Dad) don't arrive there at the same time.

You can bet that those soldiers appreciated the ride. Two outfits from this field are going to the west coast of Calif. sometime soon. I will not be among them. This squadron is the oldest flight outfit on the field. As long as there is a "Turner Field," the 95th S.S. will remain in Ga.

The inside of our office has been plain bord siding, with the two-by-fours showing—like the inside of a garage, except that the ceiling is covered with beaver board. They took a blow torch and scorched the wood. It looks nice now. It looks something like the acid burned wood in the El Rancho at Gallup.

The grounds are really beginning to look like something too. Gravel walks, lined with white painted bricks, will really make the grassy plots look pretty. Good fertile soil has been hauled in and this summer we will really have a beautiful place. The number of the squadron is layed out on the lawn in front of the orderly room in white painted bricks. Yours truly has gotten out of all the extra landscaping work so far. I'm an office man now, you know.

Do you remember how the carbon black plant in Guymon looked on the outside? Do you remember the asbostos shingles that covered the outside? Well, we have the same type of buildings here. Our roofs are covered with tar paper. At Jefferson Barracks the buildings look like old barns—no paint, just weathered old boards. And it really gets cold up there. Borden describes some really cold weather they are having up at Chanutte, too.

By the way, his address is Pvt. B. F. March, Flight D, Barracks 399, 7th S.S., Chanutte Field, Ill. He is now an instructor in magnetos, I believe he said, and ignition. Also, he is a barracks chief, whatever that is. I guess he just sees that the barracks is clean. He has no rating yet, but I guess he'll get one soon if he's an instructor.

I hope you all get to move inland when you do move. Dad, do everything you can to get a permanent appointment. You would probably stand a better chance of getting to stay in one area permanently. Wish it could be made Dallas or thereabouts. I would have less trouble getting a flight there than anywhere else—with the exception of Shreveport, La. Flights go there nearly every day.

I'll have some pictures (one portrait) to send sometime in February. This month I've been busy paying off for last month. I may just go ahead and have them made, then pay for them on the first. That way I could send them at the first of the month. Otherwise I may have to wait another month. I have the same trouble that I had at home, at school, and in Amarillo . . . I can't seem to keep any money for more than a day or so . . . a nasty state of affairs. Oh well, if I spend it today, I won't waste it tomorrow!

Well, I'll wind this up. The Lt. just strolled in again. He may misunderstand my attentiveness at this machine for work. But I do need the practice, witness the mistakes in this letter (?).

Love,
Hal

* * *

January 24, 1942

Dear Folks:

Well, here I am again, getting older and wiser by the minute. Someday, I'll learn to expect nothing then, I'll never be disappointed. I still can't find out anything about furloughs. And it looks like I'll never get to go to Army Technical School at Chanutte. But at that, I guess this field is o.k. I like it here, the people and country. It will be a hole to be in this summer, tho.

I am selling my camera—the one I bot in Amarillo. It doesn't take such good pics, and I want one that will be simple to operate, and get good pictures too. There are lots of things I want to have a record of, for memory's sake. This summer, when the trees have their foulage (?) leaves and everything is green, I should be able to get some beautiful aerial shots. I can have something to show Jake Sproules, Bill White, etc. in the way of pics. I have the material (subjects), now if I can just develope the ability.

Some of the boys here that own cars, are doing their best to sell them now. They can't get tires for them. Dad, the way you and mom drive, you will have good tires for recapping. Don't, whatever you do, let some guy trade you some other tires already recapped (or new tires for that matter) for your old ones. If you get recapped tires, be sure that you see the condition of each tire INSIDE FOR BRAKES and make certain, before they are put on the car, that you have YOUR OLD TIRES replaced. Some guy will make you a good price for other tires and they won't stand up because they weren't fit to be recapped in the first place. You always have taken care of your tires, and they will certainly be in better shape than someone elses. Be sure that you keep them. Here, they are charging $8 for a tire that I wouldn't put on a Model "T" Ford. A good recapping job on your tires will last as long as a new tire would, and will cost about one-third as much. And don't make the mistake of having your tires "regrooved" (Isn't that spelling terrible?). Regrooving may cost the inside of the casing to break, making for a pinch in the tube, or a blowout. But you already know all that . . . just don't let one of those Frisco tire salesmen unbalance your better judgement.

When this war is over, I think I'll try to buy one of the smaller, training ships that we use, not at this field, this is an advanced flying school, but one of the basic training ships, found at the beginners school. They have some nice two places, biplanes put out by Stinson, Waco, Ryan, and some Talor Craft (Cubs). Nearly everyone is going to have a plane, know how to fly, or how to service ships when this is all over. The plane will be like the car was after the last war. We will have the facilities for mass production of some of the small planes, which will keep the price down, unless a bunch get together and maintain a high price (witness the auto mfgrs. today). Here I go on politics again. I guess I'll never make a good soldier.

At last we have our "Day" Room fixed up. It is a recreation building. We have copies of nearly all of the picture magazines, the Post and lots of others. There are writing desks along one wall. Round tables are used to play games on. We have all kinds of games, mostly donated by Coca Cola Co. (Checkers, Bingo, Chess, etc.) In one room of the building, there is a new pool table and a ping pong table. It's really a nice place to kill a few hours, when it's too late to go to town, or you're too tired to clean up.

We also have an outdoor basketball court. Equipment, a basketball, football, soft ball equipment, is bought from the squadron funds. Then, for the whole post, there is one building in about the center of the barracks that is equipped for boxing, has a punching bag, heavy bag, gloves, mats, etc. But of course everyone is too lazy to use anything except the chairs in the "Day" room.

In the barracks, each man is issued a steel cot, two wool blankets, a heavy wool comfort, pillow, two sheets and pillowcase, a foot locker, and mosquitoe bar and netting (in the summer). Each Thurs. we turn in our soiled bed sheets and case, and are issued clean ones. When our shoes need repairing, they are checked in to the supply room. They are sent into town, where a civilian repairs them. If they are beyond repair, we are issued new ones. When we wear out sox or shorts, or anything expendable, we turn it in and are issued new articles. (Everything but toilet articles—which we were issued when we first went into the army. We replace them ourselfes.)

Everything must be hung up, placed in the barracks bag (a blue denim bag that looks like a big tobacco sack), shoes shined and placed neatly in a certain spot under our beds, beds all lined up, footlockers dusted and lined up with all the others, beds made, floors swept around each individual's area, windows clean and dusted, and (Have I omitted anything, Mom?) EVERY MORNING. (All shoes have to be shined and laced to the top, the barracks bag must be closed and tied to the end of the bed next to the wall. Everything in the footlocker has its place and had better be there when we have locker inspection).

Every month we have a physical inspection that is complete. Teeth, eyes, nose, throat, feet, chest, heart—everything is checked. Do you think I was as careful of myself in civilian life? I have learned a million things, some of them small, but all together they are a help in one way or another. If I ever have a son, one hitch in the army will come after he's had his college training. Borden told his folks the same thing. Anyone with any sense at all, can see that they are benefitted by this conscription. But yet, you hear some draftees griping about a heck of a place it is, what swell jobs they had to leave, how much this war is costing them, etc. You would be surprised at the number of geniuses we have among us. I can't see how this country is getting along without the civilian services of some of these draftees. They raise so much hell about everything in general, that usually they get the easy jobs and the enlisted men do the dirty nasty work. You'd be surprised at some of the things they can find for us to do! I am, often since getting this office job I've missed all the dirt, except K.P. and Room Orderly occasionally. So I can't complain about that!

* * *

January 26, 1942

I received your letter of 22nd. You say that Mac is a banker in the navy. Is that the Mac who has been renting our house? If so, have you rented it to someone else? Suppose someone wants to rent it for less than the Macs were paying? Do think that the added wear and tear on the house would be worth the little help you would be getting from the property? Or, are you going to rent the house for what you can get out of it? I was just wondering that's all.

Mom, how about another box? It doesn't have to be elaborate, just a box with something to eat in it. I saw a cartoon somewhere, showing a soldier at home during mealtime. He had his plate piled high with food. His mother asks, "And son, is the food much different in the army" . . . end of joke . . . or had you noticed?

I wish I were out of the army right now. Dad, you and I could make a fortune selling "black-out" bulbs. We would have two kinds—burned out bulbs, and bulbs painted black. That just goes to show you that I have an opportunist mind, whether I use it or not.

Well, I think I'll join the underground balloon battalion. In this God-forsaken, mosquitoes, fly, knat, snake, etc., infested swamp we fear a submarine attack more than an air attack. I guess we'll have to fight off attacking subs with anti-aircraft guns.

As for the operation—I'm well again. It's all over. I had no trouble at all. The surgeon did a good job, I stayed in the hospital for 8 days, then came out to duty. It's all healed now, except in one or two small spots. In another week (by the time you receive this) I won't even know that I had an operation. Several of the fellows had real trouble with the same operation. One guy was in for 3 weeks and couldn't get around as well as I. We got out on the same day.

I am getting to see some real ships now. When this war is over, I'll have some nice tales to tell. Some of the fellows are taking pics, but I'm afraid I might get into trouble so am not taking any shots of the real ships. I'll try to get copies of theirs. But you can find pictures of any of our ships in the newspapers, magazines, etc. I saw one article showing all about one ship. Yet WE CAN'T TAKE PICTURES! THEY CAN TRUST THE AMERICAN PUBLIC, BUT CAN'T TRUST US!!! Isn't that something! They keep the darn things guarded; we can't even board the ships. We go to some magazine to find out about the ships we see sitting about 100 yards from where I am right now. I can walk within 50 feet of them, but must get no closer. If I were to show up with a camera, I'd get shot. I mean that actually as well as literally! I'd be sure to get shot at, anyway!

Mr. March has recovered from his operations and is back at work again. Got a card from Mable thanking me for my letter? I'll write again after payday, when I'll have some stamps . . . Still am behind in Xmas Card thank youse (why not spell it that way?). Several hundred English Cadets arrived recently. This field will be a replacement center for them—like Jefferson Barracks was a replacement center for enlisted men. Met one cadet that knew of the country around "Near Ely" but didn't know the folks . . .

There I go, trying to tell it all this time. You may have reason for complaining about me not writing often enuf, but certainly haven't the nerve to say anything about not making them long enuf!

Take care of yourselves . . . believe nothing you hear about this field, or anything that concerns me, until I verify it . . . don't worry about me, I'm safer than you are, and I'll be here for the duration.

Azever with love,
Hal

P.S.: Tell Doris that she'd better learn how to treat blisters. Since taking this office job, my hands have gotten soft and velvety. When I come home and start doing the spring planting on our estate (real-estate) I'll need some first, second, third, etc., and final aid for my hands, back, and feet.

* * *

Jan. 31, 1942

My Dear Mr. and Mrs. H. W. Yorke:
(Parents of Cpl. H. W. Yorke)

This is to inform you that your son, Little Harold, has been raised in grade from private to non-commissioned officer in Uncle Sammy's Army Air Corps. The victim, your son, is resting quietly. Think of it! Fifty-four bucks per month! And now all I have to do, is, sweat out a sergeant (?) rank, n believe you me, that's just what I am doing, too.

It all came as a surprise to me. I was assigned only Jan. 1, you know. Before that I couldn't even make first class private, (Pfc.). Now this comes up. If I am shipped south of here, Valdosta, Ga., I'll probably make Sgt. So look me over! Am I proud?!! You tell me! Tell Doris that she can have an officer (or almost. Non-com. will always do in a pinch) take her to the show, when I get to see her again. If I can just go to school now! That would make everything perfect. I'd like to make Sgt. frst, tho. You can't make anything while you're there. Witness Borden. He's been assigned to Chanutte Field since about July 15. He is just what I have been. So I want to get as high as possible before I go to school. Boy! Am I happy about anything . . . everything . . . I don't hate nobuddy . . . WHAT A WORLD!!!!

I went downtown today, Jan. 31, and had some pics made. Because of my financial condition, which is as usual, I can only send you all one pic for the three of you. Divide it up. I had two large ones (large in cost, only 5 x 7 actually), made, and three smaller ones for my fans. Grandma will get one, with the stipulation that she show it to the other kin. I am also going to take some snaps of self in coveralls, cpl. stripes (that's corporal, in case you haven't been following me), and everything.

Plez excuse if this letter doesn't make sense. I'm almost shocked out of my right mind. I just heard the good news about my promotion, and I had to write, even if I am in no condition to make sense!

Write me from now on, Cpl. instead of Pvt. Don't forget that, for Pete's sake. Let 'em think that everyone expected that all along and is already use to the Cpl. Maybe another slip of the pen will make me Sgt. Here's hoping!

Went into town today and went thru the newspaper plant. They have a shop as well equipped as the Amarillo News-Globe. The population of Albany is 28,000. It's really a swell place. Much like Cuero, that is, the people are very friendly but it is very much alive. I believe I told you once that they have legalized gambling here. But none of the scum collects like you find in many places like that. It's really a clean little town.

I met a girl here in Albany on Xmas Eve nite. Since then I've either called her or seen her every day, or nite, if I didn't work. I have her snowed under, but the trouble is that she just about has me snowed under too. She is 20 years old, no beauty, but pretty, and actually, she has a mind of her own. For about the thousandth time I am being taught to dance (an accomplishment I haven't made as yet). I am not spending much money on her—she is attending a beauty school here. Living with some friends of her family, and knows that I have little money to spend—and as I said, she has a mind and can realize those things.

But, she's not the one. So you can relax again. I am still "Bertish" about marriage. When I find someone that's as conceited as I am, I might find the right gal . . . someone with some college, money, influential friends, etc. (Does that sound like Dorothy Fisk? I can remember when she had such ideas, and look at her now, poor thing.) But I'm in the army right now, or had you heard? Any soldier that marries is a [____censored____], and I don't care who he is. There are several aspects to the thing that might make you sad if I mentioned them, or do you follow me? But, I may find the gal that will make me not mind so much being a [____censored____]. Until I loose my good sense, or get out of the army, I'll have no Mrs. parked in front of my name. It doesn't belong there! (Okay, okay, Mom, I am an old woman . . .)

What brought on this tirade? I dunno. It all began with me sitting here doing nothing, working an X word puzzle, and someone came in and telling me that I made Corporal. You see, that's all it takes to get me started.

I wish I could see you all, that goes without saying. I keep saying it tho, because I hear that "wishing will make it so." I am not homesick, as the word is commonly used, but I'd give up my front seat in Hades to see you, even for a few hours.

I am making a flight to Shreveport, La. sometime next week.

I will try to find Bill D., but I have lost your letter with his address, so I don't know what luck I'll have. How about sending it again? Now don't worry, I'm already back to the field . . . As you read this, I am writing another letter telling you all about the trip. I had a heck of a time finding Bill, but . . . Hay! Wait a minute I'm getting ahead of myself. I'll leave next week. It's a very common trip, from a good field, to a good field, and in a better ship than you see on the airlines. And the pilot is a Capt. Soooooooooo . . . don't worry! I'll stay there at Barksdale Field for about 3-4 hours, only long to say hello to Bill, if I find him.

Well, this is enuf for now. Write when you can. It doesn't need to be a long letter, or about anything. Just so it's a letter and deals with something about you all. A trip, your thoughts, news from Mable, John R., anybody . . . anything that will make up a letter. Witness this mess. It's a letter (spoken very lowly and defensively)

Cpl. Hal

No need to be formal . . .

I got a card from Norman Wilmeth today. He's at Fort Benning, Ga., about 80 miles from here. Also, he's a 2nd Lieut. Got the rank from his years in the Natl Guards. Probably Starkey boys would have done the same thing if they'd had the education. But they get the rank easily, and can loose it the same way. If I could pass the eye exam, I'd have made application long ago, and have gotten it too. If they keep lowering the physical standards, I may try it yet.

I'll have been holding up on the letter so as to make sure about things. It would be most embarrassing if I should send word home, have you write, and have the rating wrong . . . On the envelope where everyone could see!

I'm sending a bit of a story I found somewhere—the second sheet.

Write soon . . .

Love,
Hal

When I was in Amarillo, I got my suit coat. I got back to the field only to find that we could no longer wear civilian clothes. I have had mine hidden in the bottom of my footlocker, hoping I'd not be caught. Feb. 3, an order came out letting us wear them again. You should see me sport my new suit. Thirty minutes after the order was released, I was on my way to town. You'd be surprised as the sense of freedom that comes from wearing the old civilian clothes. I think that I may be able to change back, after getting out of the army, if I ever do!

Do you remember the leather mesh shoes (light tan in color) that I have in Guymon? Do you know where they are packed? Where? And how can I get them here? They'd really go nice with my blue slack suit, which I already have here. This summer I'll be trying to figure out ways of staying cool. What better way than to wear cool clothes?

About one month after I get my first increase in salary, I'll be able to send you all some money. But I need the 30 bucks every month. Life is too sweet to waste it all being broke. Did I explain that in 4 mos. I'd get $10 raise for having in my year? And did I tell you that the gov't. is putting a bill thru to raise our pay another $10? I should be drawing $64. Within 4mos. which won't be hard to take!

* * * *

Postmark: Jan. 24, 1942

Typed letter

Dear Folks:

I just received Dad's letter saying that I'd probably be sent to Panama. Just between us two, you and me, I definitely will not be sent anywhere. Is there any plainer way for me to say this? I will not be sent anywhere! This is a training base. We are shorthanded here. Three-thousand soldiers will be shipped in here just as soon as barracks are built to accommodate them. I will not be sent anywhere. Your boy has had a rare stroke of luck in being stationed here at Albany. It is bad, in that I am so far from you all, but then you can be reasonably sure that you will see me some time. That is much more than lots of parents can say. The army needs men here in the U.S. at the bases. This is a base. I am needed here. Logical?

I believe I've already told you about the enjoyable Xmas we spent here—teaching British cadets to fly. I worked all day. The same will hold true on New Year's Day. We are all working seven days a week, twelve to sixteen hours a day. If hard work will win this war, we have already won. Apparently we are making up for the superiority in numbers of the enemy.

Received the box! And what a box! You forgot shoe polish and hair oil. I didn't miss anything else tho. I'll bet there is an interesting story to be told about the package of matches. There was one package. Was it an after-thought? You all must have stayed up nights, dreamed about the box while sleeping, to think of all the things you had in it. Grandma and Bert sent a box. I had cookies, candy, and a couple handkerchiefs.

Ethel Lee and Cloyde (How do you spell that?) sent a card with two handkerchiefs in the same envelope. Cards came from May, Ethel, and some others but none from Mabel, Walter or Wincie, Alice, or the rest. Have you heard whether or not A.J. is in the army?

I forgot to tell you about the dates in the box. They lasted about .3 of a second. They were the first fresh ones I've ever tasted. Believe it was for everyone else, too. I like them just as well as I do the others . . . better, in fact. They are softer and have a better, datier flavor. I'll get to read the books when I go to the hospital again. Already read the Bob Hope book. It's really a scream.

45

Mother, I appreciate your advice and opinion about my marriage. There is one thing that I don't want to happen to me. I don't want to accept the philosophy "Eat, Drink, and be merry, for tomorrow we may die" that seems to go with wartimes. The only trouble with that philosophy is that you might not die—then you're stuck. Because that idea may be sub-consciously guiding me, I think I'll wait and keep looking for a while. Maybe financial matters will improve. Maybe lots of things will change for the better. It's a cinch they won't get any worse!

Now, won't you all stop worrying? I am in no danger. I'll not be shipped out of this country. I won't even consider marriage until I find a prospective wife. Have I forgotten anything?

Well, I had better close for now. Oh yes, our officers have warned us, I'll pass it on to you for what it may be worth. "Believe nothing you hear over the radio or read in the papers." In other words, only a government notification can be believed. That and what I can tell you. But often the spot news is incorrect. A report was out here about Frisco being bombed. Very interesting! The story was denied later. The same thing may happen out there concerning this territory. So believe nothing unless it is verified by the government.

Love,
Hal

* * *

Doris:

You imp! Sending me a Christmas card like that! I spent the whole day Christmas trying to get to the card. I'll fix you! We really had some rain the other day. It rained for two days and nights without ceasing. One night we were all gotten out of bed. A hurricane was expected and we were told to hold the planes down. Honestly, we have to sit on the wings and tails when the wind gets up. But after we all had gotten out of warm beds into the cold wind and rain, word came through that the wind would only be about 25 miles per hour at its height. Were we mad!

Love.

* * *

Postmark: February 7, 1942

I am very enthusiastic about army life! We lie around in bed every morning until 5:00 o'clock. This, of course, gives us plenty of time to get washed and shaved, dressed, make our bunks, etc., by 5:10 and by 5:15 to stand reveille. After we are reasonably chilled, we grope our way through the darkness to the mess hall. Here we have plenty of good, wholesome food, consisting of an unidentifiable liquid and a choice of white or rye crusts.

After gorging ourselves with this delicious repast, we waddle our way back to the barracks. We then have nothing to do until 11:30, so we just sit around and pick up all the cigarette butts and matches within a radius of 150 feet of our barracks. Each window must be vigorously massaged each morning.

Soon the sergeant comes in and says, quote: "Come on out in the sun, boys." So we go out and bask in the beautiful sunshine. Occasionally we seek a high spot where we can remove our hip boots to empty some of the water out of the top, where the scum collects. (Bits of debris stick to you when you walk, so you must keep your boots clear of this.) To limber up for the day's work, we do a few simple calisthenics, like touching your toes with both feet off the ground, and grabbing yourself by the hair and holding yourself out at arm's length.

At 5:00 we put on a light pack and start walking to the mountains. The light pack is not to be confused with the heavy pack. The light pack includes a gun, bayonet, canteen, mess kit, coat, cartridge belt, first aid kit, pup tent, stakes, pole, and rope, and the gas mask. The heavy pack has a toothbrush included. Carrying my light pack, I weigh in at 321.001 pounds (immediately after a haircut). (I weigh 201.01 without the pack and immediately after having my hair cut). So you can understand our enthusiasm at the promise of a day of romp and play in the mountains . . . in the sunshine.

An observation car follows us as we nimbly jump from one craig to another for the purpose of rescuing those of us who are too distantly related to the goat to derive benefit of its sure-footedness. The boys who fall out in the mountain climbing are treated well. They get six months in the guard house, but don't have to face a court martial.

At 12:00, those who can, limp to the infirmary. Here the patients are divided into two groups: (1) those who have athletes foot, and (2) those who have colds. (Did you realize that every sickness can be classified in one of these two groups? I didn't either, until I got into the army.) If you have athletes foot, you get your throat swabbed out with iodine. If you have a cold, you get your feet swabbed with iodine. If you try to receive treatment for any other illness, you are sent to the guard house for impersonating an Officer.

Well, that's all right now. I've got to dash madly to mess hall. We're having hominy tonight, oh boy, oh boy. Besides, I pull K.P. tomorrow.

* * *

February 9, 1942

Dear Folks:

I am almost afraid of my own shadow! I lay awake at nights, worrying about what might happen the next day! When I sleep, dreadful night-horses (female) interrupt my peaceful slumber and all because things are going too, too perfectly! Yes, it looks like my luck is just too good to last.

Today I was ordered to report to the classification bureau tomorrow, in order to take a test (mathematics) to determine my qualifications for going to school. I happen to know that this field is shipping a bunch off sometime in the very near future. What if I get to go! That would make things too nearly perfect. If I make Sgt. the first of next month, I think that I'll run off somewhere and hide! I'll bet it will be a great big let-down when my luck does begin to fall off. But, then, I have had a lot of luck since I've been in the army, and all bad! Maybe this is just making up for that—maybe I've already paid for my good luck which I am now having.

In one way I have already paid for my good luck, monetarily, I mean. In my usual blundering way of caring for money, I misplaced $10 that I had been saving. Figure it up—10 bucks from the 30 I have been making doesn't leave much and is quite a loss. But by the time you get this letter, I'll have had another paycheck and be over the hump again. This next pay is really going to fix me up, I hope. The guys all say that the more you make, the more you spend, and the deeper you go into debt. I know that I had as much money when I made 21 dollars as I have now, making 30. "But this is going to be different" . . . heard throughout the world every day, spoken in every language known to mankind. (Confidentially, I couldn't be any worse off than I am now, if I were on relief . . . or even if I weren't on relief.)

I haven't been writing anyone, so consequently, no one is writing me. I haven't received a letter for about three days now. Guess I'll have to thunk up sumpin to write and get a few letters off, or I'll be black-listed throughout the States.

And the 14th is Val Day. Woe is me! You see what I mean when I say that I have nightmares? I'll have to write, and tonight, too. Fine war!

My corporal stripes haven't visibly changed my status in the army, or even on the field, but inside, I feel much better. And that $24 a month raise won't be hard to take. It's very moraleizing, to say the least.

You can't tell it from this letter, but my typing is really improving. I can type much faster than I could at first, and usually, I don't make as many mistakes as I did.

Well, if I think of anything else, I'll add a rider, like the insurance companies do.

Rider #1: Mom, if you are wracking your brain trying to think of something else for that box, send a pk. of needles and about 3 rolls of thread, white, black, and khaki in color. I don't have to mend my sox, I found out. When they get holes in them, I just check them in to supply and get new ones. I got them to issue me 5 prs. of cotton sox, 4 prs. of wool sox, and 5 prs. of cotton shorts, all extra so that I have to pay for them. I also got two black ties. The total cost . . . $4. I skimped thru on those things in civilian life, I'll be CENSORED if I do it in the army where I can get them cheap, and can charge them on next months pay, too.

#2: How much money did you pay Sears in Amarillo, before you got thru, Dad? What correspondence did you carry on with them?

#3: One nice thing about the corporal business is that I got out of Kitchen Police, Room Orderly (Captain of the Barracks

Sanitary Engineering Department), and all of the other details that made life so unbearable, for us privates ... oops! I mean for those Yard Birds, those privates.

This must cease.

Lovingly your son,
Hal

* * *

Postmark: February 10, 1942

Dear Folks:

Well, my intentions were o.k. I went down and had the pictures taken and paid for them, but now the guy tells me that he has to take them over. He ruined the pics in developing. As soon as I get some decent pictures made I'm shaving the moustache off. It takes too much trouble to keep it trimmed and looking half way decent.

On the day that I received your letter, Dad, with the remark that I could take care of you when I got to be General, I found my name on the list as making corporal. I still have a long way to go, but I have made the first step, anyway. I have been delaying mailing my letter, so that I could see the order concerning the promotions before I told you it was so. It's official now!

It really rains here. When it starts it comes down by the buckets full. In about 5 minutes, everything is flooded. Five minutes after the rain starts falling, everything is dry again. This sandy soil sops up the moisture. Our mud consists of sandy goo, red in color that comes off the shoes easily. Up at J.B., St. Louis, Mo., they had mud that was mud. It was regular gumbo, like south Texas. You couldn't even scrub that stuff off. Once it was

51

on, you just put the polish on top, after the stuff had dried, and polished the whole mess.

Unofficially, we will be getting furloughs in about a month. I heard that about 30 percent of us would get them at a time. But, and here is the rub, they are only 6 day leaves! But if I get one, I'll get to Calif. in that time, then worry about getting here. I believe that I could get a plane ride easily, if they knew that I would be A.W.O.L. without it. Here's hoping, anyway. But don't go and buy a ticket with the United Airlines, round-trip from Albany to Frisco. You know by this time how these rumors are, when they concern anything G.I. (gov't issue).

It's been a long time since I wrote last. Guess you all are getting pretty worried. What has delayed me is waiting for the order concerning the ratings. I got Moms letter with the stamped envelope, then later, the post cards. But where is that wallet, the military set, the stationery (if that is what Stewart sent me). I can't thank him for his gift until I receive it, can I (?), etc., etc., (and I hope there is lots of that).

* * *

Postmark: Feb. 14, 1942

Dear Doris:

It looks like this brother of yours is going to be one of those "rover" boys. I get into the army at Seattle, Wash., and finally end up in Georgia. Now it looks like I'll go to Ill. for about four months to go to school. When I get out, I should be an airplane mechanic, a "greasy monkey." Maybe we can save our pennies and buy a crate of our own.

Think of it! We could cruise over Guymon Main Street, find a parking place near the show, wave to Mom and Dad and tell them where it is, let them park the car, then we'd not have to walk so far to the car after the show was over. How would we get there without walking? Well, you could bail out, and I'd . . . Hey! Wait a minute. Somebody would have to come out to the airport to get me. I don't want to have to walk. I'm always getting gyped. Well, o.k., I'll walk!

After school, if I do get to go, I'll be shipped back to Turner Field, unless I get hooked into staying at Chanutte as instructor. Maybe that is where my luck will run out. Everyone tells me to make grades just high enuf to pass. If you make high grades, they will keep you there, and there is no way in the world that you can get out of it.

So Saturday was Valentine's Day! I'll draw you one. And it won't be Government Issue, Government restricted, etc., etc., etc.

Think of it! An honest-to-goodness original drawing by the emeenent (Mom, do something to that word, it don't look rite) artist CPL.

Harold Whitbread Yorke Junior, (Second).

If the Lieut. saw me writing a letter, when I am supposed to be working, I'd be working up from Yard Bird Pvt. again. So I'll close for now. Take care of yourself.

Azever with love,
Hal

* * *

Handwritten in pencil:
One of the dozens I've written but failed to mail—about March 3, 1942

Typed letter

Dear Folks:

Well, I've finally got the pictures from the photographer. I will mail one about the first when I'll have money for stamps. You can keep those proofs. The proof to the pictures I had made up will be sent, too, if I can get it. The photog. kept it to make the developments.

Spring is here after some pretty cold days about a week ago, and lots of rain. This bunch of soldiers is like a lot of bear cubs. We have a lot of horse play at night, a late retirer may find anything from soup to nuts in his bed—if he can find his bed. A popular sport, turning over a man's bed, when he comes in at about three in the morning. It is very enlightening—to say the least. After sleeping on these steel cots for a while, they get to look like a hammock. It is amazing to watch someone to climb into a bed that has had a broom placed lengthwise in it. Often you hear things cracked and not always the broom.

Taken all in all, the army is much like college, as far as your association with men is concerned. Each borrows the other's sox, tie, and often shoes, shirts, or blouse. Sometimes they borrow without giving notice, then some bird comes in to go to town and finds his hat, shoes, or maybe that clean pair of sox that he's been saving for a week or so, gone. As long as one man in the barracks has a dime, a fellow that really needs money can get it. They're a fine bunch of fellows, from all walks of life . . . some from good families, some from not so good. Some of them are thiefs, but the better part of them will give you the shirts off their backs.

Here at the field, we are kept pretty busy right now— especially here in the office. We are back on the 7 day week and can't get any 3 day passes. I am going to wait for a while before getting my furlough. You may get moved closer to Ga. Then I wouldn't have to waste so much time on the road. After all, 6400 miles is a long old trek. Talk now has it that furloughs will go out at the rate of 20% now, 10% a month from now, and 5% after then which of course means that even with furloughs going out, I may have a time getting one.

Never have I written Stewart, or Ethel. Wish you would mention the fact that I am getting ready to write the next time you write them. The stationary Stewart and C.M. sent was swell. And I haven't even written them congratulating them on the addition to the family. Ethel sent a card. Believe those two are the only ones I've missed, besides Alice and Harvey. Three important letters to write some day! But I am doing good; I've written everyone that I correspond with regularly. I write Mable whenever I get the chance.

Well, be sure to let me know as soon as you move. I don't want to start out for Calif. some fine day and get there and have the grocery boy tell me that you moved to somewhere in Albany, Ga. And the way I feel now, I may start out just any day.

* * *

Postmark: Mar. 10, 1942

I received the box today (20th) and I'm really enjoying it. The cakes are especially good. Everyone in the barracks came in for some of it.

I have put in for a furlough on or about March 22. Of course I can only hope that I can make it. But an order came out letting 20 men at a time go on 10-day furloughs. I am taking mine last so that I can talk for 15 days. Here's hoping!

Last week it rained day in and day out. We were almost washed away. Any morning I expected to look out my window

(I sleep in the upper bay now) and find a bunch of sailors coming down a gang plank into our barracks.

Last night I really met some swell people. They were northerns who make this country their winter resort. They have 6,840.1 acre plantation where they hunt, mostly, and raise a few southern crops. The home was the finest that I have ever been in. Very rustic, furnished like a hunting lodge. It was full of cups, pennants, pictures of prize winning dogs, etc. A big fireplace, about 8 feet across, was beautiful. The ceiling in the sitting room was two stories high. They had a bar with everything you ever heard of to drink and everything of the finest. The whole family was well educated, rich in personality, and really "quality" folk. They made the three of us feel perfectly at home.

A friend of mine, "Ham" Tom Hamilton, is very well-to-do and has traveled the world in style. He happened to know a guest of the family who was visiting these people here at their plantation. We had a formal introduction, very formal, in fact, and proper, and were treated like princes.

I enjoyed the evening so much because it was so different from any I've spent in the Army. I was beginning to stagnate, to rot in the everydayness of this soldier existence. To describe the evening in a few words, "Very stimulating."

At 2:00 war time, we left for camp. We arrived about 8:30. I hardly realized that we'd been there for any time at all. I certainly was surprised when we began to say goodbye that it was so late. It certainly was a pleasure to have to watch what I said and how I said it, what I did, and how I did it! I was really getting sloppy.

As usual, I had no money, so when we went to the show, old Yorke (Little Harold) was very interested in the comfort and safety of the helpless females. I was most attentive, so much so in fact that I failed to see that the other two guys were fighting over who would perform the honors at the ticket window. Consequently I missed out there . . . much to my dismay of course.

After the show, Little Harold suggested getting drinks in town—having already looked over the bar at the plantation.

The girls, of course, couldn't very well drink in town in public, so my invitation was not accepted and the explanation offered was that we could mix any drinks at the house. Of course I was very surprised that they had a bar! Of course! I'd have been out of luck if there had been a nice bar in town!

The people had prize dogs, horses, stables and kennels. You have never seen a better place in the movies. I have dreamed of places like this, but never hoped to see one. Everything was in the best of taste, furnishings, pictures, everything. I just can't put into the words the finery, the perfectness of everything. Maybe in trying, I made you think of the place as gaudy (I give up on that one) show place. That isn't so, it was so perfect that I just can't put it into words!

Well, I have to drop that subject, but I will never forget it. When I get my furlough, in late March, things would be favorable for me to hitch-hike out there. And don't you try to discourage me, either. That is the cheapest and quickest way. Maybe it is a little harder, but I have done a lot more work than that for a lot less money. And then too, the time saved makes it worthwhile. And let's don't make a lot of extra work for ourselves by going down and buying a ticket. It is sometimes pretty hard to get our money back. I appreciate it, don't think that I don't, but I just can't take it. It's too much money for nothing! I can get by without it.

I'll close now and leave something to say next time. Thanks for the box, again. We are all enjoying it.

* * *

Postmark: July 2, 1942

Handwritten in ink
Wednesday

Dear Folks:

I got a pk. of stationery from Mabel and pillow cases from grandma. Really nice cases! This is the paper Mabel sent, swell, too.

About the racket. It looks like maybe rats ate the strings out right at the frame. It needs restringing. But strings tight running horizontally & loose ones running vertically is what cracked the frame. The guitar will be o.k. You should know better than to take me too seriously in my ravings. Half the time I am exaggerating for the comic (?) affect.

Wilda will write you my particulars about the wedding [on June 28,1942]. All I know is that we got licensed at about 11:30 & were married at Presbyterian Church at 1:00 p.m. We went on a picnic lunch with Marches. Came back in & went to show Sun. nite. Mon. morning I was back on the post at 7:30. I had to get back for barracks chiefs meeting, to turn in the laundry, pick up last weeks, etc. I finish another phase Fri. nite. Will let you know how I made out. We set off the 4th home. It really is amazing. We didn't get off on any of the other holidays. But I'm not complaining It really will be nice to be out for 2 full days!

I'll write again when I have more time. I had to write Grandma today, besides getting lesons. That crowds me!

Write us at the new address at Champaign. It's too hard to get mail here at the post. Even when you do get some, you never know if you have it all or not!

Glad you are permanent in Seattle. That is my favorite country—there and in Oregon.

Azever with love,
Hal

Did you get our wire to 620? Linden Ave?
Sent Sunday afternoon.

* * *

Handwritten letter from family friend, Mrs. W. F. Fisk
Wednesday

Dearest Stella & Doris,

I recd your card some few days past but it has been so hot here we could not have pep enough to write. Hal & Wilda came by to see us & were we thrilled to see him & of course Wilda also. I begged them to spend the nite with us but they had to go on it just so happened that I had baked a cherry cobbler & I fixed them some. We certainly did like her & Hal said he was not going until he got to see Will & was Will thrilled to see him they strutted off out in the yard to chat alone over old days as the said did not interest the ladies. Leah was home to & she was so glad to see Hal. "I'll tell you Stella we nearly ate him up & it did Dorothy so much good you would have died if you could have seen Dot & Hal." She made such a fuss over him & they talked about what they use to do when he lived next door & Hal gave her a couple pkgs of cigs & after he had gone she said "Well isn't he just a darling." I said yes but you kept me scared to death for fear Wilda would think you were going to eat him up. He had her stand under his arm to see how tall he as. He surely has made a fine looking chap & has such a sweet personality. He made some kind of a remark & Leah spoke up & said. "Oh yes I see you are a chip off the old block" & we all had a big laugh over it. I didn't know him when I went to the door. I told girls who were sitting here with me. Here is a nice looking young man in the wrong place & then he smiled. I recognized him at once.

Well I hope you all got back o.k. I guess you enjoyed your little visit home & especially when Hal arrived. Kiss Doris for me. "I am still mad when I think of that telegram. I may fuss over it but I'll never look the same."

We had a good rain yesterday & could stand some more of it. Everything is as dry & hot. Well Stella I surely enjoyed your visit & whenever you can seize the opportunity come again & write when you can. I shall always love you & yours. Well sorry, but there are no more letters from Hal in 1942.

* * *

Postmark: Oct 4, 1943

No letter but two newspaper articles enclosed

#1:"A Parrot Story"

This small story comes to us through the courtesy of the Free French grapevine. A German officer, upon entering a village café in France, was greeted by the proprietor's pet parrot, which said: "Death to the Boches!" The German merely smiled. The next day, however, when the parrot repeated the same remark in his presence, the German did not smile. The third day, when the German came into the café, the parrot said it again. "Mort aux Boches!" This time the officer jumped up in a great rage and shouted at the proprietor: "If your parrot says that again tomorrow, you'll go to a concentration camp!" After the German had left the café, the proprietor, perspiring freely, took the cage and went to see the priest, who also had a parrot. The parrots were exchanged. Next day the German officer stalked into the café and passed directly in front of the cage. Silence. He paced back and forth; still the parrot kept silent. Finally, he stood directly in front of the cage and said, "So? Not saying anything, eh? Come on, come on,

Death to the Boches! Death to the Boches!" And then the parrot, in a suave, even voice, said: "May God hear you, my child."

—Baltimore Evening Sun

 # 2: "A Knockout by Ickes"

"In the tumult of events a recent exchange of letters between Lt. Governor John Lee Smith of Texas and Secretary Harold Ickes in his capacity as Petroleum Administrator escaped general notice," says the Atlanta Journal, adding:

The public, we believe, is the poorer for it and we make haste to remedy the situation. The Texas statesman was irked because of the gasoline restrictions which were cramping social life in his demesne and he addressed a long letter to Mr. Ickes in which he declared, among many other things: "If this is the type of intelligence directing our civilian war effort, then God pity America! The heroism of her gallant fighters is being ill repaid by the fatuous fumbling of confused and capricious crackpots who frantically and furiously confuse the home front and demoralize their earnest efforts to achieve victory."

Pretty good, eh what? "Fatuous fumbling of confused crackpots," that's getting 'em told. But don't think for a minute that "Hairbreadth Harold [Harold Whitbread Yorke]" was dismayed. On the contrary, he swang (as Dizzy Dean would say) from Port Arthur with this haymaker: "As you go vociferously forth, draped in the outer garments of patriotism and the underwear of self-interest, please remember that our tanks and trucks and Jeeps cannot burn as fuel the crocodile tears you shed in resisting the non-necessitous consumption of gasoline." Score it as you please. In our book it was a knockout by Ickes.

* * *

Postmark: Dec. 1, 1943

Guymon, Okla.
Dec. 1, 1943

Dear Folks,

I'll try to write a few lines at this time. Everything is pretty calm at this time. We have a "No Visitors" sign on the door because of Mother so there is no confusion at home.

We arrived in Guymon at 1:00 P.M. Saturday. Earl's [Wilda's older brother] funeral was held Monday afternoon.

It seems that Earl had started out in the country to get Mr. Roust to fix his gun for him as he wanted to go hunting Thanksgiving Day.

John Gable, a young boy who had worked for him, was with him. It seems that they were going down a hill and undoubtedly swerved to miss some object—perhaps a car as they saw cattle tracks there—and lost control of the car. Earl had a 1940 Ford he purchased in Sept. The patrolman said they probably were driving about 45 and then, too, on a downgrade.

Both Earl & John got their necks broke. Earl was mangled horribly—so bad it was necessary to practically rebuild his face. As I understand it, John wasn't so crushed & bruised up. No one will ever know exactly how the accident happened. Dad had an attack with his heart the morning Earl was killed. He was advised by the doc to stay in bed but Dad wanted to go to the funeral so badly. He got up a little Sat., then he stayed up a little Sat, then he stayed up almost all day Monday. He just overtaxed his heart talking too much and trying to keep up so long. Mon. night at midnight he had another heart attack and died then, Tuesday at 12:45 noon.

Perhaps this will be another shock to you because I don't believe we have ever said anything about it. Mother is pregnant and is expecting in January. Therefore, this double tragedy is very hard on her. The Dr. has advised to keep her quiet so there has been the minimum of any callers this time. At Earl's death there was too much confusion and the people mean well but don't help at times like this.

I plan to stay with Mother until the later part of January at least. I hate to be parted from Hal and I know he hates it too but I feel this will help Mother a lot.

Dad's funeral will be Thursday afternoon. The sooner it is over, the better for Mother's nerves.

Here it is Thurs.—everything is o.k. thus far. We got your telegram, Dad. Thanks for the offer of help. It is a very big help, just knowing that you were tracking us. Don't believe that we will have to call on you tho. Money matters will straighten themselves out eventually. Right now we can handle everything.

I advertise in the Guymon paper to sell the car. Am asking $950 & don't believe I'll accept less. Am afraid of the tires, had to buy a battery the day of Earl's funeral but a light, cheap one & it doesn't work so good. Then, too, if anything should break down, we couldn't possibly get parts, or afford them if we found them. Carl Hunt called last nite. He's interested, he sed. I plan to go to Amarillo and try for a X country hop toward Ga. If that isn't possible I'll hitch-hike back. You know, I know the way.

Wilda has to stay here for a month or so. We'll probably get together again around Feb. or thereabouts. I will try to buy another car at Albany & have it fixed up before Wilda returns.

Earl's car body was a total loss—tires, frame, fenders, are all o.k. Ford said he couldn't fix the car at all, so guess Ins. will pay "total loss." Wish that there were some way we could get that motor & the tires to put on some car that I may pick up somewhere.

I got a 5-day extension on furlough. Had 14 days, so don't have to be back until Dec.15th. Will leave about the 9th or 10th to be sure to get back in time.

Put the guitar back in the m. room. The rentor sed the roof leaks in D. room. Then too, the mice are getting bad. Told Mrs. D. & she sed something about using candles to fumigate & get the mice. It is impossible to get a carpenter, I'm afraid. The leak has stained the wallpaper, but doubt that it is hurting anything too much. The leak is at the door to the living room, just inside D. room. Mice haven't hurt anything of ours. Some got into their chair, but not too much damage resulted—must have been a little mouse.

* * *

Postmark December 1, 1942

No letter but one newspaper article enclosed
"Wonderful Snow Covers Panhandle—Sergeant Burns up in Midst of Panhandle Blizzard"

Sergeant Yorke, of World War 1 fame, was a sissy Staff-Sgt. H. W. Yorke, Turner Field, Ga., and former Guymon, Okla., resident was speaking. "Us Yorkes seem to get into trouble whenever we go but he had Germans to fight in the last war. I had a panhandle blizzard."

It all began the day before Thanksgiving when Yorke's brother-in-law of Guymon died. The Sergeant and his wife drove from Georgia for the funeral. The following Monday they were in Amarillo at the home of friends, Mr. and Mrs. Clyde March, 3911 Polk Street, when word came that Mrs. Yorke's father had died.

Last Thursday they started to Guymon. That was the day the blizzard came swooping in.

They made it as far as Uncle Bud Crawford's ranch, two miles south of the Bivins Booster Station when the car stalled in a snow drift. With the Yorkes was a Mr. Feltz of Dumas. There was nothing to do but wait for rescue parties. It was bitter cold and growing colder. One could not see the front of the car from the driver's seat. It was unthinkable to try to walk to safety.

As they waited the car grew colder. Light overcoats used in Georgia didn't seem of much use in this freezing temperature. Then they remembered they had a case of motor oil in the back of the car. That could be used for fuel. Sergeant Yorke took a hub cap off one of the wheels, poured oil into it and lit a match. They had a stove.

This was 12:30 Thursday afternoon. They kept comfortable through the afternoon and night. Other stranded motorists dropped into her car from time to time to "heat up." Everyone was cheerful. One man suggested a diary be kept in 10 minutes intervals, but Mrs. Yorke overruled this as being "too much like a last will." The blizzard grew worse with each hour.

Finally the Yorkes dropped off to sleep. At 4:30 Friday morning, Mrs. Yorke awakened her husband and asked him to refuel the oil pot. As he poured oil into the hub cap an explosion threw burning oil all over the soldier's face, arms and clothes. He was a human torch.

Using presence of mind, Sergeant Yorke jerked opened the car door and rolled into the snow to extinguish the flames. He was a mass of blisters. The car was blazing.

Smothering the car flames with overcoats and snow, the rest of Friday morning was spent stuffing snow down into the car's upholstery and pulling burning cotton from the seat cushions. The pain grew more intense for Sergeant Yorke.

At one o'clock Friday afternoon, 24 ½ hours after they first stalled, help came to the rescue.

U.S. Helium Plant workers were attempting to get to the North Plant. They made it as far as Yorke's car. Coffee, piping hot, and lunch kits of the workers were opened up for the stranded and injured passengers. Then the Helium bus turned around and pushed the soldier into Amarillo for first aid. Mrs. Yorke went to Guymon by train.

Sergeant Yorke left Amarillo yesterday to his Georgia base. His face and arms still a mass of blisters.

"I wish I knew the names of all those who aided us," he told a Globe-News reporter. "They are the finest people I ever met. I especially want to thank Johnny Raef and a Mrs. Ann Hooper (Hooper was her maiden name. He couldn't recall her married name) for bringing us into Amarillo for treatment. She didn't mind my silly looks a bit. She bundled us up in her car and took us to Mama and Papa for help." He calls Mr. and Mrs. March Mama and Papa because he grew up with their son, Lt. Borden F. March, while a kid in Amarillo and Guymon.

But not a single time did he mention a certain barbed wire fence supposedly to exist between here and the North Pole. He said he was grateful for being alive.

—*Amarillo News*

* * *

Handwritten letter

Amarillo, Tex.
12-12-43

Dear Folks,

A lot has happened since I wrote you from Guymon. So much in fact, I feel like it all took place years ago. After Dad's funeral I'd decided to stay with Mother until her baby was born. Hal didn't sell the car so he finally decided to leave the car with me and hitch-hike back to Georgia. He helped Ann, Earl's wife, inv the stock at the station on Monday & Tuesday, and on Wed. Dec. 8th I drove Hal to Amarillo. (Oh yes, here is some bad news for you. Hal wrote a check for $60 on you before he left Guymon). He spent Wed. night at March's place and planned for Hal to leave early Thurs. morning and I'd drive back to Guymon. It drizzled rain all Wed. night and then turned to sleet and snow early Thurs. morning so Hal said he'd drive me back to Guymon and go on and drive the car to Ga. We started from Amarillo and about 18 miles south of Dumas we got stalled. There were several big trucks and cars stuck on the highway and we couldn't get by without getting stuck and couldn't turn around. So there we were! The wind was blowing too so we were in the middle of a bad blizzard and no way to get out. We were stalled about 12:30 noon Thurs. About 2:30 Hal drained the car so it wouldn't freeze and took a hub cap off, put an ash tray in it, and knotted up a handkerchief and used some oil we had in the car and started a fire. Naturally there was a lot of soot and smoke involved. About 8:30 that night a truck (we had a case of oil in the car) from the Bivins Station came down and was taking people back (we were about 2 or 3 miles from Bivins). They stopped about 300 yds from our car. Two or three men were trying to drag people against that north wind to the truck and then we weren't guaranteed the truck would make it, so since Hal and I were warm at least we decided not to leave our car. Several people stopped at our car to catch their breath and they were half-frozen. One old man of about sixty decided to share our fate and stayed in the car all night. We heard next morning that they had to work half the night with two of the women who went to the truck. They were almost frozen. At least we stayed comfortably warm—even though we looked like Negros from the smoke & soot. Anyway we got along all right until 4:30 Fri. morning then the oil got too low and started a fire in the car. Hal grabbed the hub cap and threw it in the snow He splattered oil all over him. He rolled in the snow and then grabbed his overcoat and threw it over the blaze in the front seat (we had our stove in the front and had the front seat on the floor in the back so we had almost a bed in the back and the three of us had used Hal's overcoat as a blanket. I had on Hal's woolen underwear & wool socks too) then Hal started handing the old man snow to throw on the fire. (Oh yes, the wind had stopped blowing about 12:00 midnight.). He got the fire out with a slight damage to the back of the front seat. Of course the car is sooty & black. We started our little stove again and stayed in the car until 10:00 when some man came from Bivins and said a truck with a heater was warm so we went back to the truck—which was loaded with oranges so we enjoyed a few oranges. This was the first thing we had to eat since Thurs. morning—we had a candy bar with us but that isn't much. In a short time some people who were on their way to work at the Bivins Helium Plant came by in a bus. They got hot coffee out of their lunch boxes and gave us that. (Mr. Feltz, the old man, was still with us.) The workers decided they couldn't make it on to work so they turned around to return to Amarillo so Hal and I went back to Amarillo with them and did we look like a couple of negroes—I should say three because Mr. Feltz went too. In Amarillo two of the workers got their car out of storage and took us to March's arriving at 1:00 p.m. Friday we changed clothes and Hal went back to town with our dirty ones and also to see a doctor. (Hal's face was burned on the left side—not deep but a nasty-looking place. His right hand had two rather bad places.) The Dr. treated the burns with sulfathiazole ointment (sp) to stop infection if any and said they would be all right. Saturday afternoon Mr. March and Hal went back for the car. Snow had drifted in all around the engine so a truck hauled the car 30 miles to Amarillo making no charge!! The man said he wouldn't charge a soldier anything. Hal got the car running again and cleaned a little of the soot off and started back to Ga. at 12:30 Sunday noon. He has until 8 p.m. Dec. 15 so I think he will make it okay—if not, he can always wire for an extension of time. (Another change of ink—I started this letter in Amarillo after Hal left and I got a ride to Dumas so I am in Dumas now and hope to be in Guymon sooner or later.)

I caught a cold and feel a little rotten but don't believe it will be bad.

I have tried to tell the complete story but don't know how I have succeeded. Excuse all the errors because I don't feel too good. I think everything will turn out all right. In day or two I'll try to write again.

Lots of love,
Wilda

* * *

Handwritten letter
12-15-43

Dear Folks:

Guess Wilda told you about all our trouble.

Blew out another tire returning to Ga. I managed to get new tire made of reclaimed rubber. Looks good. My fire insurance will pay for our upholstery & finishing the inside of the car—I hope. I am supposed to see the adjuster tomorrow.

I got back here at 8:30 a.m. on the14th & had to go to work at midnight that nite. Drove straight thru without sleep—42 hrs. then didn't get to bed until 2:30 p.m. 14th. Slept to 11:00 p.m. & then had to go to work. Got in at 8:30 this morn & slept to 1:30 this aft. Can't seem to sleep much!

Hope you are all well. Mom, that car of yours really is cutting up. Maybe you should go to where it won't bother you so much.

I had to borrow $60 Dad, but should be able to repay you before Xmas. I am not spending much money here for food. I buy milk & bread & eat up what we had stored.

I'll write when I get a little more settled.

It has been snowing all day—most unusual, old timers say. Take it easy, Doris.

Azever,
Hal

* * *

Handwritten letter in ink
4-15-43

Dear Dad:

We've been thinking of you a lot lately. I'm sorry that I had to delay so long in writing. This won't arrive until a day or two after

Sunday. But Dad I had to be sure! Maybe our news will make you forget your disappointment in not receiving this letter sooner.

Wilda has stabbed me in the back. She consulted the stork, without my knowledge, and made arrangements for a visit from him sometime in January. A G.I. doctor told her we could expect a little bundle from heaven about that time—and he didn't mean pennies, either!

Think I'll insist on Univ. of Tex. & suggest a medical career.

Golf balls are hard to find. A jeweler here plays golf—I've asked him to get us some. I'll get the golf balls, but they may not be such good ones. I know pre-war quality is a thing of the past. The golfers here are having trouble with the war balls. The covers come off & the balls are dead they say. But they'll do to stay in practice—mebbe.

My bad foot is a little better. Guess before it's all over I'll have to go to a civilian doctor for treatment. The place isn't bad, but worries me, being on the bottom of my foot.

I put in for a July 1st furlough, but won't know if I'll get it until about June 25th. Could you get off on such short notice? I'll wire when I know for sure—unless I find out in the next day or so.

I'm enclosing a letter from Clinton. Thot you mite like to hear from him. Plez return the letter.

Wilda took the fountain pen to work with her, so Ill close with a pencil.

Wilda tried for golf balls at a store in town—she had to describe the ball to them, they haven't seen any in so long! Sed they weren't expecting any, either. But we'll get some somewhere if they're to be found.

Gotta go now.

Mom, the doctor gave Wilda a thoro physical already, including a blood test. Before the baby is born, they take Xrays. She is given about 14 days in the hosp.—all for free. Will write more about it next time—tell it all now & won't have anything to talk about next time.

I put in for a new time—need the certificate to take along on furlough just in case!

er, with our love
Gotta go.
Wilda & Hal

How's Aunt Doris?

* * *

Handwritten letter in ink
5-20-44

Dear Folks:

Serious I haven't been trying for a furlough—in fact the R.C. informed me here that they could swing an emergency one if I wanted it. But I know of no way to make such a long trip—unless it was absolutely necessary. From the R.C. report, & your letters, mom, I decided the trip wasn't really necessary.

But we were worried. Mr. Bender had us all fooled—none of us knew how his illness was, even when Hayes repeatedly warned us. I was afraid you might be placing too much emphasis on how much better Dad was each day, in your letters.

How would you feel if Wilda wrote, told you I'd had a heart attack a week before but was getting along alright now. Then, in letters following, tell you I was much better today," his breathing seems so much improved." We were in Guymon at Mr. Bender's bedside when his breathing was labored. With such a vivid picture before us, surely you can't blame us for being nervous and seeking definite facts about your condition, Dad.

By the time you receive this, you should be feeling yourself again, Dad. But for crying out loud, take it easy for awhile. Believe I'll get the R.C. to check for us again to find out what the doc thinks now.

It really is a lucky thing you went to a doc, instead of trying to let nature do the work alone! And thank goodness you have confidence in him and follow his advice!

This Sun. we've been informed we won't work, come hell or high water.

The men are getting stale with so much work & so little time off. It doesn't take long to show up in our work. (We see to that!!) So, if possible, we paint the car.

I went swimming out at the post pool yesterday—11:00 am. to 2:15 pm. Absorbed too much Georgia sun—have a little burn today, but not so bad. I enjoyed the new exercise a lot. Wilda & I will try to go in after we paint the car—if it isn't too late.

Dinner's ready so will close for now. Haven't anything to say, anyway.

Sun. evening 8:00 pm. Went swimming this afternoon. I got up too late to go to church, tho. Both of us are sun burned a little—nothing serious tho.

Enclosed are a pic of the car & one of the motorcycles. Also is a slip giving my new classification? It's the highest rating an enlisted man can get. Of course lots of guys have the same rating—but it it's still the highest possible rating. I've had the rating for over a year now. But only recently the ratings above 750 were done away with, leaving 750 tops.

Wilda's ready now, so will close & fix an envelope!

Loads of love, of course—
Azever with love,
Wilda & Hal

* * *

Handwritten letter in ink

5-20-44
5:30 pm

Dear Folks:

Answering Mom's questions . . . Right after the war, the "date of discharge" was set at "duration plus 6 mos." After each 3 years, from the date of enlistment, we receive a 5% of base-pay, longevity, tacked onto our pay. After June 12th, I'll draw present pay, plus 5% of $96. (About $5) After 6 years, I'll get 10%, 9 years, 15%, etc.

Mom, one of the best army jokes is the question, "Are you going to reenlist?" There will be no furloughs between enlistments. Prewar, after a hitch, a man was allowed 30 days to make up his mind about reenlisting. The 30 day "furlough" wasn't really a furlough, & didn't count furlough time. In other words, you were allowed 30 days each year for furloughs. You could save up time on your last year & take a 30 day furlough, wait 30 days to reenlist, then get another 30 day furlough for the first year of the new hitch. Do you follow me? I say that was possible, technically. Actually, the guy was lucky to get the full 30 days between reenlistments (army red tape, filling out papers, etc.).

But as I sed, reenlistment is all done on paper. We can't reenlist. Everyone is in "duration plus 6 mos."

But, being a regular army man, I'll have opportunity to reenlist, ahead of the present draftees (Supposed to, anyway!).

We surely are glad to hear that Dad is taking up normal duties again. And, in a month or so, you can play a little golf occasionally, will feel the whole incident can be forgotten.

Sunday, if possible then, we'll make another stab at painting the car.

Tuesday nite we took some newly graduated lieuteinants to Atlanta, Ga., about 165 miles from Albany. We left at 6 p.m. Got back at 2 a.m. & went to work at 7 a.m., arising about 6. We carried 4 men & their groups for $10 each. Had good luck, no flats or other trouble so cleared $35 cash. And when the next class graduates, you'll find "Little Harold" there asking if anyone wants to go to Atlanta!!

Found out something about our car that I didn't know before—we have an overdrive. With O drive button pushed in, you have free-wheeling up to 32 miles per hour. At 32, the higher gear (overdrive) slips in, & you are not in "freewheeling." In overdrive, the car is pretty sluggish on the hills, especially with a load. Going to Atlanta, rather than lug the engine, I'd let the car drop down to 22, where O drive falls out. (You're in regular high with freewheeling then.) & then I'd pull the hill easily enuf!!

Well, I found out yesterday that there is a way to get the car out of overdrive without slowing down. Just press the gas to the floor, a switch at the carburetor throttle lever is tripped & the car slips back down into conventional high! After pulling the hill, on passing the car, or whatever, just take your foot off the gas completely. In a second you feel the car go back into overdrive. Simple, wot? And to think I've been driving the thing all this time without being able to figure out what that little push switch on the carburetor was for!

Andy Dean, 3 ½ mos. old, weighs only 17 ¾ pounds. Must be starving to death in Guymon?! Mrs. Bender, Rheta, the baby, Ann, Harold Ray, & Leona [Wilda's family] are all doing well.

I'm going to try for a furlough about July 15th. Dunno how we'll come out under the new set-up on furloughs. When I do get my next one, I'll have to wait 1 yr. before I'll be due another.

Gotta go now. Wilda is doing my work for me while I write (drying the dishes).

Azever with love,
Wilda & Hal

* * *

Handwritten letter
5-25-44
5:50 pm.
(I finished up the dishes!)

Dear Doris:

Well, kid, how are you doing now? I guess you and mom are glad to get Dad to work again and out of the way, so he won't be cluttering up the house! That's had an moral, you & Mom seeing Dad sitting around, taking it easy, while you work all the time.

Do you all have a camera, can you get film, if not, what size do you need. Sometimes a shipment comes into Albany. We stay on the ball & get #127 for Rheta & our camera. I could try to get some for you all if we know what size.

When I picked up my cadets to take to Atlanta, one of the boys gave me a pair of shoes. They were torn up, but in the army, a pair like that are the same as new ones—we can turn them in for a new pair. So I got a new pair of shoes, no ration stamp required!

If I can ever catch an officer friend in the right mood, & I have $3.50 with me, I'll get Dad a pair of officer's shoes. They are plain, round toed, low-quarters with laces. Should wear well, I dunno.

We are fighting cuts now, in addition to knats, roaches, flies, & mosquitoes. I only hope we don't get any more bugs, other than the above mentioned insects. At the post bed bugs are about to carry the boy's off. One guy was waked up the other nite by a bed bug that was trying to find his dog tags to see what type of blood the guy had! Wilda does our laundry now, so we may miss the epidemic until they get things under control again.

One of the boys at the post swore that this actualy happened: He sleeps upstairs in the barracks, & one nite he woke up & two bed bugs were carrying him down the stairs. One slipped & made a little noise—the other sed, "Ssssh, you damn fool, you want to wake up the big bugs & have them take him from us?"

And now I gotta close & get dressed. Going to Atlanta we filled up with gas here, & then, just outside of Atlanta on the way back, we filled up again. The guy ran a little bit onto the ground, but considering that amount too, we had used only 9.3 gal to go 173 miles, averaging 19.1 miles per gal, driving 55 miles per hour, with a big load! I want to fill up now & see if we did any better coming back, empty. Of course I've already made 2 trips to the field, lots of stops to go, but the average should still be pretty good! We drove back in 3 hrs. 20 minutes, 165 miles. (Got pretty good tires, only one recap on the ground, & it's a 6 ply, factory recap—best tire we have, I believe!)

As I sed—gotta go.

Azever, with loads of love,
Wilda & Hal

* * *

Postmark: June 1, 1944

Handwritten letter in pencil

Dear Folks:

Well, it really is hot this aft.! This morn, I had to be on the field at 7:45 to shoot a rifle for a score. I got 147 out of a possible

200, which is about average, but still not so good. I get a little comfort from the fact that we had to use a "peep" sight instead of the open, sport sight which I am accustomed to use. The score qualifies me as a "marksman" (127 or over). Sharpshooter has to have 150 or over—expert, 172 or over.

Sun. at River Bend, 3 of us fellows were playing around in the water. Today all 3 of us are excused from calisthenics. One has a broken toe, another a torn muscle in his shoulder, & I an infection in my foot! Guess we'll stay in the shallow end from now on & play with the other youngsters!

Zagnit, the other inspector, working with me on the AT-10 line, is going on furlough tomorrow—which means I'll have the whole job to do alone. It really isn't much, but then anything is too much during the summer! (For me, all the time is summer time!) Have a chance to make several hundred (round 4) if I can get it painted & sold in a week or so. One fellow has a 40 Ford, good shape, wants $750 for it. This is Ford country—can get around $1000 cash for it 3 days after I buy the thing. I found a 35 Pontiac with 5 pre-war tires which have lots of tread yet and a 41 Stud 6 (medium-sized) for around $800. Hope to sell our Stud for around $1,000, buy the Ford, fix it up & sell it at profit & buy the Stud to keep. Buy the Pontiac & take the tires off for the Stud—sell the Pontiac for $450. With the tires that are new on the 41 Stud.

Now don't blow up! But at first I thot I'd try to borrow the money to buy the Ford—thereby getting things to roll. But then we'd have 2 cars on hand & that would not be so good if I should ship out! God willing, we'll make some money this month & end up with a 41 Stud. With good prewar tires! (The Stud probably needs rings, rod inserts, valves ground, repaint & some touching up—cost about $25.) But that stuff is our sweat!

More wishful thinking? Okay, we'll see! If the present deal doesn't work out (someone buys the cars before I can get the money together) there'll be others. When we do sell the present car, we'll have some money to play around with.

Payday

Well, went out this morn at 7:30, finally got paid at 11:00. Came in home and am signing off now.

Azever, with love,
Wilda & Hal

* * *

Handwritten letter in pen
July 6, 1944

Dear Mom & Dad:

Things being as they are, we can't be with you when you celebrate the anniversary this month which marks 30th of such milestones. But you know our hearts are with you, and we are thinking of you on that day.

These thirty years have been full ones. There have been awful tears, but there have also been some wonderful tears—and the happiness has more than overbalanced the sadness. The important point is, you have shared that life for all of these years—thirty of them!

We want to wish you continued happiness in the years to come. I hope we can contribute something to that score. After 27 years as a pain in the neck, it's about time, don't you think!

In his mail we are sending you a package. I hope you get it Friday 14th. We hope you enjoy it as much as we enjoy sending it to you!

Wilda has completely recovered from her illness. She returned to work yesterday. We are hoping that nothing else will happen now.

I'm enclosing a letter from Stewart, that maybe it would be more up-to-date than any you might have from him.

Borden was forced down at San Diego, Calif. account of engine trouble. Don't know if he is on his way or not—he didn't (& of course couldn't) say. He did say he was expecting some excitement soon—and had already had some! But it doesn't pay to read between the lines—his next letter will probably come from Clovis, again.

Wilda needs a little help straightening out this dump—so will stop for now.

Azever with all our love,
Wilda & Hal

* * *

Enclosed in same envelope postmarked July 6, 1944

Dear Doris:

Mom & Dad are now members of a 30 year old union—quite an accomplishment! Anniversary this month which marks the 30th of such milestones. But you know our hearts are with you, and we are thinking of you on that day.

These thirty years have been full ones. There have been awful tears, but there have also been some wonderful tears - and the happiness has more than overbalanced the sadness. The important point is, we have shared that life for all these years—thirty of them!

We want to wish you continued happiness in the years to come. I hope we can contribute something to that score. After 27 years as a pain in the neck, it's about time, don't you think!

In this mail we are sending you a package. I hope you get it Friday 14th. I hope you enjoy it as much as we enjoy sending it to you!

Wilda has completely recovered from her illness. She returned to work yesterday. We are hoping that nothing else will happen now. I'm enclosing a letter from Stewart, thot maybe it would be more up-to-date than any you might have from him.

Borden was forced down at San Diego, Calif. Account of engine trouble. Don't know if he is on his way or not—he didn't (& of course couldn't) say. He did say he was expecting some excitement soon—and had already had some! But it doesn't pay to read between the lines—his next letter will probably come from Clovis, again.

Wilda needs a little help straightening out this dump—so will stop for now.

Azever with all our love,
Wilda & Hal

* * *

Enclosed in same envelope—Letter handwritten in pencil
Wilda & Hal
Dad: We sent a cashier check to Gean for $60., asked him to send you the deposit slip—o.k.?

Thanks for being so patient with your delinquent subscriber!

* * *

Typed letter
Albany, Georgia

Dear Dad:
Enclosed is a letter, which I hope will settle once and for all the post-war problem of rehabilitation of yours truly. I would

like for you to read the letter as if I were writing it to you and let me know if it is satisfactory. I am not making application for the job itself but merely trying to get them to ask for personal information about myself and tell me what the possibilities are in the job. Do you think I have interested them enough to bother with me?

I know that if we can get an offer of a good business without too much cash outlay, you will be interested also. This seems to me to have possibilities for a business, which will not only include the dealership of a darn good car, but which may also incorporate within itself a business of automobile accessories and even household appliances in time to come. Of course, Studebaker dealers service cars as well as well as sells them.

I wish you would let me know right away because this is not the only attempt that I am going to make to have something already lined up for us when our present jobs are ended.

We may not get the dealership in Guymon but they may offer a similar dealership in some other locality. I spoke to a Studebaker dealer here and he told me that in several cases Studebaker was willing to furnish a building and even parts, tools and accessories to start a business. If this should be the case, then a large capital would not be necessary, but in any case it costs nothing to investigate.

I also wish you would make suggestions of editions or better wording of the letter enclosed. I will wait to hear from you before doing anything else.

Azever,
Hal

* * *

9-13-44

Dear Mom and Dad,

It has been definitely settled for us that we'll spend this furlough here in Albany. I don't mind it so much, the reasons being so good, but am still sorry we couldn't make it to Guymon while you were there. But the war can't last forever, & when it ends, we'll be together again.

Davidsons really have been nice to us. It is impossible to ever repay such kindnesses that they have shown. It seems that they are on hand to help every time something comes up—and they act as if it were the most natural thing in the world for them to put themselves out for us. Be sure to give them our regards—as well as our thanks!

Wilda & I are recovering from a Ga. summer cold. We were both feeling pretty tough for a while. Wilda had 5 teeth filled on the right side of her mouth & the doctor used shots so he could speed up the work (I guess that's the reason for the shots). Anyway, Wilda has been running around like she had a load of chewing tobacco stuck in her cheek. I expect to see her spit toward a corner at any minute. But most of the swelling is down now. She has more teeth to be filled! —on the left side.

Clifford Pafford is still somewhere in the Med. and has a motorcycle—he had one, but has gotten another one, a better one now on board with us. Plans to use it when & if they get to port & get to stay there long enough to get shore liberty.

Stuart wrote that he was very busy "helping cupid's vitamins." Wonder if he ever found any of Dad's folks? He never did say anything about it to us.

I'll close for now. Hope the sale of the business is going well. We'll let you know when the machine arrives.

Borden was thru Guymon enroute to Platt. Hans couldn't write you, but called Mrs. Bender.

Azever with love,
Wilda & Hal

* * *

10-31-44

Dear Folks:

I've changed jobs again. I am now a post inspector. In addition to insp. every plane on the field once a month (175 B-25s) (50 AT-10s), we also look at all trucks, cars, tugs, and spend one day a month in P.L.M. (where I've been working). My new hours are 8 a.m. to 5 p.m.—no night work. We have a separate squadron, only 13 men in the squadron! We get furloughs every 6 mos. now, so I can definitely plan on a furlough about April 15 or May 1st if Wilda & "whatsit" can travel by then.

This is the first time in my life that I've really felt secure—especially since being in the army. I am now assured of a permanent station here on Turner and know I'll be here when Wilda's time comes. Beyond that, I really don't care!

Wilda has finished the first 3 lessons on her correspondence course. They really are a lot of work, too. Believe she is going to make the grade in fine style.

The kids are raising cane around the house & Wilda is interrupting to ask, "Remember wat we did last Halloween nite?" And I don't remember so well probably—she reminded me, she baked her first cherry pie, we went to a party at a fellow's place. He has since shipped out.

We haven't played any bridge for a week or so. We've gotten into the habit of going to bed at about 8:00 p.m. & are beginning to yawn by 7:30. It is 6:55 now, and I'm ready to call it a day!

Got paid today, drew 17.50 for 2 mos. pay. Some of the boys were standing around at noon time, playing poker. I was counting my money & accidentally (?) dropped $1 on the table. Five cards were dealt to a spot in front of me. So I played them—10 min. later, I went to work with my $2 plus $17. It's the first time I've ever won anything to speak of. It really comes in handy at this time. We are planning on ordering baby clothes sometime next month.

Hope you are thru there, Dad, by April. We are going to drive to Tex. on furlough about then. If I have to make the trip in a model "T."

I'm gonna keep that promise. And I mean that! We will get another 25 days for Seattle of course. Tomorrow I'm going to the commissary (G.I. gro. store) and buy up a month's supply of groceries. We save about ¼ on most things. Cigs. are ž.20 ctn. out here, cost $20.00 in town. Jellys, canned goods, etc. run about the same. Pots. & fresh vegetables cost about ½ at the commissary.

I am trying to talk Wilda into giving tools for Xmas. We can give each other wrenches. That way, when & if we buy a car, I'll be able to do more of my own work on it than I could do before. But she doesn't seem to like wrenches. You can see why I haven't written sooner. I can't seem to keep my mind on anything long enuf to finish up the job. I've started several letters, but always put them aside before they're finished. A few days later, I find the letter, & begin all over again. Believe I'll send this one regardless.

Wilda is washing dishes so will stop & go help her. The washing machine is a blessing!!

Azever with love,
Wilda & Hal

* * *

Dear Mom & Dad:

I am having a time writing this letter. I've started 4 times, this is the 5th attempt. It seems that I can't put my thoughts down on paper.

The last few letters we've received from you have shown complete reversal of your forever attitude towards life. Heretofore, you have been afraid to plan—afraid to enjoy the sunny days because a cloudy day was bound to appear sooner or later. I surely am glad to see that you are planning on some happiness ahead. In your letter, Mom, you said that you believed in the prenatal influence. I can't say I agree—but then I can't set myself up as an authority on the subject, so I won't disagree either.

Wilda is taking the course for several reasons: (1) to make use of idle time, (2) to continue her education (3) and to accomplish something which she had looked forward to, and hoped for, for a long time. I am taking the mechanics course for much the same reason. Only my course costs nothing, and I stand a chance to learn something else that may help to iron out some of those wrinkles in my brain.

Wilda got very nice house-coat, a red wool flannel affair, trimmed in white, with a belt. It's long, almost touches the floor.

Glad to get the pictures. It's been so long since I saw some of those kin, that I had a time recognizing some of them—A.J. & Stuart, namely. I'm returning the pics that you want to keep. I'd like to have one of Stuart, Carrie Mae, & little Stuart (How old is Stuart Jr.?) Back to the robe: Wilda got it at Sears, one of their best. She needed one badly. At the hospital is where it will prove its worth.

You see, it's this way—Wilda will be in the maternity ward with Tech Sgt. Whatsit's wife (grade higher than I) and she mustn't show anything but the best in clothes. If she does we will be ruined, socially, & won't be able to get T-Sgt. Whatsit's wife to stay with Harold W. III. Sometimes when we want to go out, she won't want to associate with poor trash! Wilda has some nice things to take to the hospital. I'll have to wash every night when I get home from work, but will get by. Mrs. Bender sent Wilda the nicest bed jacket you ever saw. The furniture in the nursery is just like the rest of the stuff in the house— cheap, but clean. It isn't someone else's dirty stuff cleaned up. I thank goodness the baby won't remember all this—he surely would think of us as a couple of cheapskates. About the washing machine—We certainly don't expect to keep the machine. You are just as interested in getting by cheaply, as we are. We can buy a machine from Sears on a monthly basis, just as easily as paying cash for one.

And that reminds me. We have stopped buying on credit from Sears. We figure this way: we have the cash in the bank, it draws no interest. Why pay Sears about 10% for 3 mos. (40% yearly?) for "borrowing their money" or "credit," name it what you will— that sounds like Andy's Grants 400% to Grimes! (Remember?)

I am laying linoleum in the baby's room. It is in Albany, but the freight depot hasn't delivered it yet. Guess I'll get a few more grey hairs trying to get the stuff to fit in the room. It measures 98 x 11-3, with a 2 x 46 closet. Like this, guess I'll go nuts no matter what. Wilda is getting along very well in the correspondence course. My lessons in auto mechanics have not arrived yet. When they do, I'll educate you on Pontiacs—one of the best. (I know, I've changed my mind.) If we can buy a Pontiac 6, I'll be very happy! Which reminds me—is the present car a 6 or an 8? I'm pretty sure it's an 8. My book shows it to have 103 h.p. etc., etc., etc.

If you are fairly certain, Mom, that you won't be using (Oh Lord, something else!) the machine, we'd like to have it now. But I plan to install one of those kits to make it electric, Mom, if it's o.k.

by you. Think I can find such an affair for about $15. Well, let me hear what you think about it. We may play a little bridge tonight, so will stop & help Wilda straighten up a bit. Bye for now.

Azever,
Wilda & Hal

* * *

11-22-44
54 Wm. Binns
Albany, Ga.

Dear Folks:

In a way I'm sorry to hear of the new job coming up. If you're ready to retire, mebbe you better do it now, while you can still enjoy life. That country out there is a heck of a place to live!

But if you can hang on for another couple of years, mebbe prices will drop to where you can buy a nice little place and still have enuf money left over to fall back on in case the chickens go on strike.

Dad, you should have lots of vacation time saved up. Couldn't you take off for a month—call it sick leave, if necessary—and make a trip here to Ga. in easy stages of about 3 one thousand mile relays? We may be able to find some kind of car & we could meet somewhere in south Tex., where you could get in some golf & fishing, both. We will get 25 days to go to Seattle. That would give us a nice visit together. I suppose, at best, it will be March 15 or April before Wilda can travel. So we could half way begin planning on some kind of get-together. But we still have to find some kind of spot.

Time to go to work—gotta stop.

Sometime later—

I got home to find your Xmas gift here. It will come in handy—you know that—and we give you more thanks than can be spoken. We have tried to get a few things each month, so as to protect the bank account as much as possible. Xmas & all the other expense during December would have certainly drained heavily on our resources.

If you refuse to retire, Dad, I believe I will. I'll just stay in the army, let the govt. clothe me, & depend on your "gifts" to pay incidentals. Nice racket!

This marriage business is better than college ever was! In college I sometimes had to ask for it!

We still play a little bridge, usually 2-3 times a week. Wilda & I had low score only one night since we've been playing. And that nite we won only 1 game in 3 rubbers—couldn't get any cards. But we aren't good! Night before last, Wilda bid 2 and made grand slam. A few rounds later, I did the same thing—bid 2, made grand slam. I don't mean we opened with 2, but that's where the bidding stopped. Each time our hands were split up so that neither looked better than a 2 bid. We play contract, so you know how we felt about the deal. The first time we only lacked 2 to win game & rubber (60 p.t.) & were vulnerable.

One time we were vulnerable, & the other couple doubled my 5 bid. I redoubled. We made it. That was delicious revenge! One night they won all the rubbers but we had high score for the evening—got it by setting them so you know what kind of bridge players we are. Guess you'd have a big time watching us—like watching 4 clowns! But we'll learn!

Supper is about ready so will stop for now.

I am trying to catch a hop to San Antonio some weekend. Would like to drop in on the folks in Cuero (& San Antonio, if I had time) even if it were only for a couple of hours. I'd leave here Sat. morn. Arrive in San Antonio in the afternoon, & have to leave there about noon Sun. They have a limit of 78 hrs. on a "cross-country" pass. Of course if you are weathered in or the ship is grounded for mechanical trouble (heaven forbid!!) we'd have to stay longer. I'd only have to notify my C.O. & the pass is automatically extended. What is Walter's address? John Rohre?

You shouldn't feel old—55 & 57 are not bad. There's a Cpl. here on the field that's 52 and he takes exercise, marches in formation, and works with the rest of the guys. And the army is supposed to be tough.

You don't want to get the wrong impression from my letter wherein I told about getting 17 bucks for a 2 buck investment. It's no habit. I match for cokes, flip nickels, etc., but never play for any high stakes. I have never dropped any real money. But on payday, if I draw an odd $2-$3, I'm sometimes tempted to give it away. But I usually come out with my money, plus the fun of playing for a couple of hours. I never quit ahead, unless the other boys stop. But when I get back down to my chips, I walk out. But such goings on take place only on "company" time (duty hrs.) and rare occasions when the interest in watching becomes too acute. I know, "quit watching!" Simple solution for another 24 hrs. In case of mechanical trouble, if I couldn't talk the field's transmission crew into doing the work without me being present, I'd be stuck with the job. I'd be lucky to get help on the job! But usually nothing serious happens, only a 10-15 min. delay. In case you get weathered in, you are grounded until sky's clear from your present location to another field which is in line with your destination. If you're unfortunate enuf to have all & good instruments for "instrument flight" & a pilot that wants to return to Albany, you can go on thru. weather, if it's clear where you expect to land.

I gotta stop!

Wilda sez to tell you not to expect a big baby. She is trying to keep her weight down to a doctor's prescribed approximately 25 pound gain throughout the time.

Azever with all our love,
Wilda & Hal

* * *

Thurs. 25th Jan.
54 Wm. Binns

Dear Folks:

It's 6:20 p.m. now. Can't see Wilda until 7, so will drop you a line in a letter—which will beat a postcard.

They let me in for a minute to see the baby and Wilda just now. The kid has black hair, weighed 7 pounds 15 ounces. This morn when I sent the wire, the doctor only guessed at the weight, the baby hadn't been weighed yet. I forgot to say on the telegram that the time was 10:15 a.m. But I guess you could figure that one out yourself.

Wilda woke me at 3:00 a.m. morning of 24th. She had been having pain since 10:00 p.m. She had had no sleep at all—I had about 2 hours. We called a city ambulance, they came right away, and we got to the hospital. (The ambulance service here is free in the case of an emergency.) The details of what followed aren't very clear to me now, thinking about it. Wilda had quite a time of it tho. Finally, this morning, the doctor had to use instruments. But all went well. The medico did a swell job of it.

Last night, they kept Wilda under dope most of the time. I stayed right with her, of course, and she did some very funny things, now that I can see the funny side. Once, she started looking around the bed, I asked her what she was looking for.

She said she had dropped an open safety pin. I told her not to bother, I'd get it. She dozed right off again.

Tell Doris that I suspect that she was wishing for a girl. Her wishes were stronger than mine. They overpoured me! Seriously, and you know how it is, Mom & Dad, when the kid arrives, it makes no difference whether it's boy or girl—just so it's arrived!

I'll drop the cards every day. I'm writing this so I won't have to write a card tonight. As soon as Wilda came out of the ether, she said she was sleepy—of course after asking me whether it was a boy or a girl and how much it weighed, and told me to go home and get some sleep. I arrived at the house and went to bed at noon. I didn't wake up until 5:30. Got up, dressed, and came right out here.

Azever,
Hal

P.S. This baby is very smart—already! She will accept no substitute—refuses the bottle. They used instruments delivering, but left no marks that we could see.

* * *

There are no letters from Hal again until August1945. During that time, in April 1945, President Franklin D. Roosevelt died and Vice President Harry S. Truman succeeded him as president.

A crippling six years after it started, World War II officially ended August 15, 1945, when the Japanese formally surrendered following the atomic bombing of two of its cities, Hiroshima and Nagasaki. Germany had already surrendered three months earlier after Hitler cowardly committed suicide.

* * *

Aug 9, 1945

Dear Stella and all:

At last I am trying to write you a letter. I have been up and down and am now just out of a spell. I am eating a meal every day and my appetite has improved. Now I want to say that I am happy that you have such a lovely home. God bless you all in it only drawback to it all is, that I cannot say it all, but God has been good to me I must be satisfied. I want to write Hal and Wilda soon. They wrote me such a nice letter which I have not been able to answer yet. Tell them if you write, why I have not written. Writing is such a task for this old lady of 89 years and I doubt if you can read what I write: I surely miss you and the evening sessions. I cannot see much, and the time is filled with other things that Bert cannot read to me every day. I will find out if Dr. Duckworth thinks it's possible if it will help my eyes to have my glasses changed. I can see objects around me, but I cannot see the fine print about my room. Bert has tried so often to get someone to do the work, everybody is too busy. I think if it was a larger job he would have a better chance. So the money is in the bank and we are just waiting. I guess you know Ethel has traded for another place, much better they say. Harvey has been operated on and we hope for good results. Mrs. Schultz is my standby. She got your letter and was so glad. She sends love to you and Doris. Bert is perfecting a water system out on the farm. Mr. Winker and he are laying pipes and making it easy to water the stock. Liza says: "Howdy" to all. All well in S.A. Tex. Little Stuart is watching and waiting for "Daddy." May the Lord send him home soon.

Well, Doris, come to see Uncle Bert and Grandma soon. We miss you all so much. Uncle Bert sends love to all three. Send me some pictures of your lovely home. Lots of love from Uncle Bert, and your loving Grandma. My best love to Harold, and may he be well.

With love and best wishes for future happiness and prosperity along with blessings and all things good.

Lovingly,
Mother

* * *

8-15-45

Dear Folks:

The good news has at last been verified! Everyone here went crazy—know it was even worse there in Seattle.

We got the enlargements—they were very good, considering the size of the negatives, etc. The baby pictures we had made were beauties! Four poses were taken. All were good. One caught Barbara with her hand moving. But the facial expression on that one is so good, we're going to have "miniatures" made from it. It will be about 10 days before we can get the prints. We got the proofs on Mon.

The field has been closed all day & remain closed tomorrow. I don't suppose we will have a lot of work to do when it opens again, and surely they won't continue the pilots training program now. We will just sweat it out until we find out what they plan to do with this field, with us and with the army. Barbara is crawling around on her hands & knees now. She has learned how to swing in her baby swing & really loving it. The affair has a spring at the top, you know.

Hope they put out some news about the size of the army, rank of the personnel, etc., so we can decide what we want to do.

I would like to get out & take a "Kaiser" auto agency. See Henry & ask if it would be o.k. with him.

Azever, with love,
Wilda, Barbara, Hal

P.S. Are any vacant lots in your part of town? How much? We want to begin spending money right away!

* * *

8-20-45

Dear Folks:

We are really busy—Wilda with the baby & apt.—me with the car. Wilda has an appointment with the doc for a physical exam for Barbara & to begin her "shots."

I have sanded the car down & resurfaced it with "primer" coat. Tomorrow or as soon as the weather permits, I will apply the blue lacquer, then hand rub it out. Quite a job, but it will cost about $15 instead of $65.

News came out at the field that men with 55 & over points are "frozen" to the States. So I won't go over until I reinlist, anyway. We have heard no news on that score either (I have 59 points, up to VE Day).

Last letter from Mrs. Bender sez that Rheta was getting along fine. If her check on the 14th came out o.k., she is probably up & walking around.

May know tomorrow what they plan to do with this field. I expect they will close up, but haven't heard the first word about it—not even a rumor!

We used a little of the magical D.D.T. insect spray on the few cock roaches we have. It works pretty good, but so does "flit" & a dozen other sprays. I think the stuff is over-rated. Really am anxiously awaiting the new Sears catalogue. Want to see all the new furniture, auto parts & tools, etc., etc.

Wilda still gets to work on her lessons—occasionally. But at the present rate she won't finish up in the allotted 3 yrs. period. She only has about 2 yrs. to go, & isint 1/3 through! It's quite a course—she'll finish it up, of course, but it surely is a lot of work!

Hope you get all settled by winter time. Then next summer you can really get your money's worth out of the new house.

You never can tell we may be transferred closer to you in a few months. One thing sure, we can't be shipped much farther away!

We have definitely decided to stay in the army if I can keep up the present ranks, which I doubt—if I can stay with one bum eye—if the present rate of pay is kept—which I doubt. But almost anything would beat Clowe & Cowans.

* * *

8-21-45

Painted on the car until I ran out of paint "thinner," then had to stop. Got to sand it all down again, put on another coat of paint & then hand rub it down. I'm worn out tonite. Hope to be threw by Sun. but who knows? Got to go to bed now—I'm really tired.

Azever with love,
Wilda, Hal, Barbara

* * *

Aug. 11, 1945
This is the lost letter

Dear Folks,

This really is nice. I'd hate to tell you what I think of the commanding officer J.B. That was really an army hell-hole. The food was rotten. The mess officer must be trying to make enuf to retire when his 3 years are threw.

Here the food couldn't possibly be better. The privates are fed with N.C.O.s (non-commissioned officers). Everything is good & served in a clean way.

Rules here? There aren't any. We don't even have to have a pass to get into town.

Albany is a town of about 20,000, small, but friendly to us. They have 4 shows & a U.S.O. recreation place. It's even swanky & home-like (USO) the ladies aid society or something similar runs the place. They are so motherly and homey it's pitiful. As the soldiers enter the door, they meet him, introduce themselves & express a hope of making him at home here. They try so hard. I do appreciate it, but it is pitiful. I guess they have sons in the army & it makes them feel better that they're doing their part— or something. Everything about the people & their attitude toward the soldiers is pitiful. It seems (here not at St. Louis) like they all think of you as a son or brother.

But now comes word that we won't be here long. Some of us will be put on the line (servicing planes) & the rest sent farther south to a new airport down in southern Georgia near the Florida line. When we do get settled permanently, we'll be sent to school as our field quota demands. But A.M. ratings are hard to get. You have to be qualified for them, take, and pass, an examination, then wait until they need such a specialist. But with the rating comes a higher rank. An A.M. gets staff sgt. rating. His pay usually runs to over $100 per mo. and ration money—if he so desires (money for food, lodging & clothing if he has a wife).

Yes, we have planes here. There are some 2 seated 600 h.p. attack planes, fully equipped, except for armament, low-wing jobs, and ordinary trainers. Also have some twin motored, 450 h.p. each motor, low wing light bombers used for navigation training (called advanced trainers), equipped for blind flying. Then there are a few bi-planes, single 450 h.p. planes, used for observation trainers -- foto +

ships, reconnoiter, etc.

Our barracks is about ½ block from the apron. At 5:30 we are wakened by the blast of about 2 score motors. At first it's just noise, but as they warm up, throttles are corked open. In about 10 minutes it's impossible to even think. After about 15 min. of this (5:45), they are cut down a little. Then, in a few min. we hear one motor rise above the others. Its thunder gradually dies down as the plane taxies down the field. Then, it rises again as the plane comes back for the take-off. When the plane zooms into the air & gets about 15 ft. off the ground. The roar changes to a blast until it rises to about 40 ft. Another has taxied down the field while I was talking about that first plane now its blast sounds & it's off. They follow like that and when the last one is off, the first is on its way down. That's what we hear all day long & most of the nite.

Nearly everyone here is an officer, a flying cadet (soon will be commissioned), or N.C.O.s with specialist ratings. Three-fourths of the others are just waiting for an opening before they become N.C.O. & get ratings. Nearly all of them have nice cars or motorcycles—or both. But they aren't a bit snooty about it. This southern hospitality is a fine thing.

Mon. I found the Y.M.C.A. here. They have a nice indoor pool, gym & all kinds of exercising paraphernalia. I'm going to enjoy that. Service men pay only for towels & soap he uses (5 cents each towel & bar of soap).

It's about 4 min. in to town. Bus costs 10 cent each way. But I've always hitch-hiked in. The people fight over which one is to stop for us.

Mom, how about writing Borden? He always mentions when you do, & he says in every letter if he received a card or a letter from you. No kidding.

* * *

Inexplicably, there are no letters from Hal again until January 1959. Although Hal and his family lived only within a few miles of his folks at times, which would explain some of this gap, there were other times when we were far away—in Germany from 1949 to 1950, in Puerto Rico from 1954 to 1957, and in Virginia 1957 to 1959. During this period, Hal and Wilda added three more children to their little family—Carol (Betty) in Georgia 1946, Harold in 1948 in California, and the fourth child, Richard (Ricky) in 1951, also in California. While in Germany, Hal worked in the Military Intelligence, where he investigated the backgrounds of German civilians seeking work with the US Army. He didn't like this work, however, because he preferred working with his hands. Later he would have an opportunity to return to the type of work that he loved by teaching helicopter maintenance when stationed in Korea for a year.

* * *

Jan. 59

Dear Folks:

We haven't heard from you in quite a while. Hope you aren't under the weather. We have had some real cold weather here but all of us are well. Wilda has one toe nail that wants to grow in—she keeps working at it and so far has kept it from getting to the stage that Doris had.

I went out to the commissary & bought a side of beef at 43¢ (plus 5% surcharge). The side weighed 378#—believe we must have gotten about 60 # of hamburger meat. The stuff wasn't wrapped, so we used up 5 pks. of freezer wrap & spent 2 hours getting it in the freezer. Don't think I want to eat any beef for a couple of weeks.

Last week I spent quite a lot of time on the platform. Had a million & one things to do after my 7 wks. at Sikorski and the holidays, but believe, Mom, I am ready to start with a clean slate. I have completed 3 of my lessons on the 22 lesson correspondence courses, have none on hand right now—probably will get 2 new lessons this week coming up.

One thing I haven't had time to do is to get the Ford advertised. Want to get that done about next pay-day (at the end of Jan.) when people have money. It costs nothing to get it advertised in the Post "Daily Bulletin" for 3 days.

Betty had a good piano lesson Fri. (one of her best). Harold is doing well on the sax. It hasn't taken him long to learn to read music & to learn the sax keys.

Thurs. nite

Wilda & I defrosted the freezer. That is a job! It only took about an hour, but we tried everything (fan, hair dryer, scraper, etc.) until we finally got the right combination. After that the work went fast.

We haven't used the stainless steel set you sent—waiting for company to come. With a freezer full of steak, it shouldn't be hard to get company here! You better begin planning your trip to Va. and set the date B.S.G. (before steaks gone). We really are proud of the set you sent. It is nicer than anything we've ever seen before—certainly we never expected to have anything so nice. Now Wilda wants a new set of dishes!

I spent 2 hours just polishing & cleaning my brass for 2 uniforms. Still, I'm not satisfied with 1 set & will work on it during next week. When I am satisfied, I will put on a coat of clear nail polish to keep the stuff looking nice. The polish only keeps off the tarnish for about 2 weeks, then the brass turns dark under the polish. Have to remove the polish, shine the brass again and paint it up again. It's a never ending process. Even bought new brand for my cap this time—went all out!

Sunday want to repair the "HO" gage (Macaklin) engine today if possible. Had a piece of the motor frame broken (it was made of "pat" metal) & had to make an entirely new piece. Have the piece now, but it is rough & has none of the holes drilled for armature & the attachment bolts. I'll have to do a regular machinist/watch maker job before I get it fixed properly.

I'll add a few lines to Hal's letter now. Thanks for the table service—it is so complete and looks so nice. We used it on Xmas day but haven't used it since.

I still have the $20 you sent to buy a formal for Barbara. Do you want me to give her the money so she'll have it when she needs it or would you prefer that I get her the dress? I hate to get her the dress really because it may not fit her when she needs it, or I can return the money and wait until she is a little older.

I have to give Barbara a permanent today. She went to the beauty shop and got a haircut so I have to give it today because she doesn't have any curl at all.

We really haven't decided about any trip this summer at all. Hal couldn't get but 30 days and our traveling time would be at least half of that time so that doesn't leave much time for any visiting—it would be so much easier if we were closer to Calif. I know that the trip is a long and hard one for you folks too but you don't have to follow a time schedule like we do. The last trip we took was 37 days—spending a week at Guymon and a week in Fontana and about 4 days with Leona but actually Leona's stop was a necessity on the trip back so I could wash & iron clothes. So you can see that 30 days only would really rush us.

I don't know what Va. schools will do next fall. Norfolk schools are still closed (6 of them). If they have the same trouble here, I don't know what we'll do. Maybe they will open a school at Fort Eustus for the military but we might have to send our kids off so they can get an education! I'm not going to worry about it yet but we might have to do something.

It is time to get busy now so I'll sign off.

Love,
Hal & Wilda

* * *

Sun. 22 Mar. 59

Dear Folks:

Well, my "vacation" is over. No more house work, cooking meals, washing clothes—well, <u>almost</u> no more housework! Now I can go back to work where a man can occasionally rest. I managed to get the front yard covered with saw dust (old) and lime mixed in a bit. Also spread Bermuda "hulled" seed which is supposed to germinate in 7 days. Of course I didn't loosen the soil at all & the high winds we get every morning has swept the packed areas bare—no sawdust, lime, or seed. If the rest of the area grows, maybe I can spot the bare places.

I have the go-cart ready to assemble. A fellow at post did a good part of the welding for me. I can do no more now until I get the wheels from Sears. They keep sending notices that they will ship when they receive from the manufacturer. Actually, I still have a dozen things to do which aren't dependent upon the rear wheels (already have the front wheels, which are 8" which are semi pneumatic—rears are 12" pneumatic). Betty, Harold & Ricky are getting impatient. The least said about Wilda's reaction, the better. She's not crazy like me.

I checked with that nearby motor court about renting a cabin by the month. They said their winter rates would still be in effect—until June 1st—which will be a bit better than 7 days for the price of 6, at the rate of $10 per day. In other words, they will let me know the exact price in a day or so but as it stands now, the price is $60 per week! Wouldn't it be better to stay here with us? The kids will be at school all day—until 3:30 p.m.—and Wilda will be here. For the kind of money it would cost to go to a motor court I can do a lot of things. I have all the screens that were at our windows when we bought storm windows and I could fix up the garage into a sleeping room for the boys. They would like that and May is the most pleasant of the months here. Of course, we still have only one bathroom and one coffee pot—the 2 most important necessities.

About Wed., I began my day/night work with the new course. I have to monitor all instructions and on April 6th must give the instruction on hydraulics. I have about 7 days, then about a week off before more hydraulics instruction comes up. Hope I can do a good job—especially on hydraulics. When this course is completed, another will begin before the end of this fiscal year—and next fiscal year we have 4 such courses scheduled. But these first 2 are the important ones to me. I am the "coordinator" on them—the others will be given the same way as other courses are handled here at the school. Each community will be responsible for their portion of instruction.

Had to have Harold's horn worked on again. It is okay now. He still is still good about practicing. We might as well give up on Betty. She's good but even the best have to practice. She is too interested in everything but piano.

Believe Ricky is improving his behavior at school. At least we've received no notes from his teacher recently. That is some improvement right there. Babs is doing almost straight "A" work—only one "B" in science. All the kids are doing well but Bab's gets the best grades. We can't complain about Ricky since he is still recuperating from skipping a grade. And Betty & Harold are doing more than school work—they have music practice to take up a lot of their spare time.

Wilda & I spent all morning just working in the kitchen and utility room. Still have more work to do there but they are improved. We want to get the rugs cleaned and the place will look a lot better, but there are so many things that need doing which we just can't get to on weekends. So far, Wilda hasn't done any ironing yet—and she has the whole week's stacked up on her!

We are all excited about seeing you within a few weeks. There will be no hot weather, flies or mosquitoes to make life miserable. Maybe we'll even have some grass growing in the front yard! But don't be disappointed if you find a nice stand of crab grass instead of Bermuda. It all has to be mowed—and I guess that's the object?

Have to stop this and join Wilda. She's still working in the utility room—looks like an all-day job.

All join in sending our love.

Azever,
Hal

* * *

Sun. 29 Mar 59

Dear Folks:

Well, I've been busy the past week, as well as this week end. I've been working with the new class during duty hours and

104

preparing my lesson material at nights, plus today. Yesterday I spent the whole day working on the go-cart. I have it about 3/4 competed now with lots to do on that last 1/4! Only big problem now is securing a sprocket onto the rear heel for power and mounting the clutch shaft properly. I'll have it completed about the time you get here. Had all the welding done at the Hull Repair Shop on Ft. Eustis with no cost to me—about $20 worth of free work! I make up parts until I can make no more (additional parts depend upon attachment of the ones I have made) then I get those added to the frame. Then back to the garage to make up the next batch. Wilda is going nuts with having everything to do about the house. The kids are little help!

Ricky was set up to have a birthday party (about 10 classmates/neighbor kids invited) and then he got sick. Seems to have the flu—is feeling good one minute & sick the next. Mon. is another Easter holiday so maybe he won't miss school. We cancelled his party & set it up for next Sat.

Betty, Harold & I got rigged out this morning and went to church. They had communion so the kids experienced that. Both said they had taken communion before so it was no novelty, I guess. Wilda stayed home with Ricky. Babs claimed she "has nothing to wear" so she stayed home, too. We ordered Harold some new shoes from Sears—found the order stuck down in a chair cushion Fri., so Wilda had to get him a pair at New Market shopping center Sat. That's cutting it pretty thin, isn't it?

Not a blade of grass has sprouted from the 10# of seed I scattered in the front yard! The past 4-5 nights have been freezing, although it usually becomes comfortable during the day—unless the wind is up. Maybe a few days of warm weather will bring out some grass. The weeds have greened up, what with the load of sawdust and bag of lime. Guess I'll have to settle on the weed lawn again this year. It will take at least a year for me to regain heart to try for more grass.

I had to swap brass to clean uniform today. It takes about 15 minutes just to make the exchange. When I have to clean & polish brass, I am working like mad for about 2 hours. Every time I touch my brass, I think of how ridiculous it is to have all that stuff on clothes I wear! Another couple of years!

Car running good, approaching 50,000 miles fast. I will hit that mark in another couple of weeks. Gotta be thinking of realigning brakes this summer.

Wilda has taken Fri. & Mon. off from work. Kids are home for Easter so she is baby-sitting. It's really nice to come home to a wife instead of bringing her home every night & have to wait for supper, find a messy house, etc. I'll be glad when she becomes a housewife again.

Thanks for your Easter card. I never think of greeting cards when I'm in the P.X.—have to remember Kleenex, etc., etc. When your card arrives, I think of it then. Ricky received the wallet and is very proud of it. He has never had a new wallet of his own. Betty & Babs hand down their old wallet to him. He sat down & went through all the compartments & card holders.

The other night when we went to New Market, Ricky stayed in the car (he got to feeling bad after we left home). He fell asleep and I started the car, running the heater. He woke up and, began talking so strangely, I thot his fever had really gotten him. He asked, "If you were dying, would you hear a whirring noise?" And he told me he felt so funny. He kept talking so strangely that I watched to see if he would pass out or something. Then I thought of the heater & turned it off and asked if he still heard the funny noise. He realized what the matter was and looked so relieved. He had been sound asleep and awakened to hear a strange sound. I know how he must have felt.

Well, it's getting late and I have to work tomorrow. One good thing about my job as coordinator on the new course is that I am getting a review of everything I had at Sikorsky. I should be well versed in the H-37 after a couple of classes, don't you think?

Wilda & kids join in sending loads of love. Be seeing you soon.

Azever, with love,
Hal

* * *

Fri. nite 18 Nov. 60

Dear Betty:

I really have mail to answer! Received a letter from Mother, one from Harold, and another from Doris! Have 2 letters of yours to answer too.

You wrote about all the work your music teacher had assigned but mother said in her letter today that the teacher had agreed to let up a bit. How do you like her teaching? Does she correct mistakes or does she just let you go right ahead and ignore them? Bet you are glad the work has lessened somewhat, anyway.

Today I had to drive into Seoul [Korea] to pick up my boss, Lt. Campbell. He flew into the airfield there, from Pusan, and I had to make the trip to get him.

Guess you all have read what Pres. Ike has decreed on dependents overseas. Some 200 thousand will be returned home. They are spending too many U.S. Dollars outside of America. Wish they'd send me home, too. I'm ready! But that kind of funny business will surely make a lot of young fellows think twice about making a career of the Army, maybe Air Force, or Marines. It means that if I stay in the Army, regardless of where I go o'seas next time, it will be without my family. If I had been considering staying in the Army, I surely wouldn't hesitate now in deciding to get out!

The cost of maid service will go up for me this month. Last month, 6 of us had one maid. Now they have hired an extra woman so that each has 3 rooms to take care of. That means that the cost will double. Can't complain because she shines shoes, keeps up the room real nice and probably will do laundry—what there is to do during winter months, which isn't much. Cleaning and pressing will be costly, I guess. Oh, well, you can't take it with you.

Wish I could have gotten pictures of the children here in Korea before I "lost" my camera. The toddlers all run around with the seat cut out of their britches—saves on laundry. The kids have no toys such as American children. (No little cars, trains, Erector sets, etc.) But many of them have tops and they are like ants along the roadside (and in the street) playing with their top. They empty garbage and sewage into the ditch in the city. In the little villes, all that is saved for the rice fields. The liquids are still poured in the ditch or thrown across the road to settle dust. The filth and stink here just can't be described in words. You have to be here to understand it. They eat some kind of food that gives off a stench that, I swear, you can see. Even the better educated and the moneyed gentry eat the stuff. I still can't stand to be in the office with all windows closed—the odor actually demands your attention. There just isn't any way you can ignore it. Mind over that matter is powerless. Lord help us when it really gets cold and we have all the heaters on full blast and windows closed! I can walk into the warehouse where they hang their coats and smell that awful rotting flesh odor—it clings to their clothes.

I ran into Lt. (now Capt.) Beason yesterday. He is a doctor, and mother and I saw him often at Capt. Galiffa's home in Puerto Rico. Col. Nothingham, provost marshal in Puerto Rico, is also here. There are lots of people here that I've known at various places in the Army. Having served in the 13th & 6th helicopter companies and in TSMA, I am meeting a lot of people in the 13 months I am in Korea. I'll be running into these guys for the rest of my life now.

Battle of hi-fi is now in session. It wouldn't be bad if it were radio and each was on the same station. But they are playing records. I don't know if I can stand 8 months more of this or not! If I come home whistling weird tunes, they aren't foreign. They're just <u>mix tunes</u> of good (?) old American music.

I asked mother not to send me any package. I just want pictures for Xmas. But she mentioned a box she is sending. I never have received the box of goodies that grandma mailed me. It will really be something when it arrives, I bet! I'll have to wet the end of my finger to eat them—like you eat salt. After losing my camera I'm not anxious to have any small object that can be "slickied." I have made my contribution to the Korean economy and I don't care to repeat the action. I doubt they would slicky family pictures!

Several of the guys send taped messages home. They sell small rolls of tape the size of 8 mm film (the film you see in the boxes at grandma's are actually16 mm. film split in half. The messages are in boxes the same size square but half as thick). It costs about 30¢ for tape and postage. They do that instead of writing letters. As much time as I spend at my desk writing, I am inclined to think they have the right idea! It seems that I have no time for anything else. I can't sit idly in my room 5 minutes without taking up a pen and jotting down a few lines. Maybe I like to write letters and just looking for something else to complain about?

Xmas party plans are coming right along. The carpenters have parts for the locomotive and coaches all cut out. The merry-go-round should be mechanically ready next week. Have to paint and decorate it. The Sgt. making the drawings of clowns, santas, etc. is really good. And I think we are going to have a very nice carnival set up for the kids. I know it will be the best they have ever had—in fact, I know you all would enjoy it very much, too. I'll get one of the guys to let me use his negatives of pictures he takes. After all, I did none of the work but the designs, plans and mechanical parts are all my brain children.

Well, the end of the 2nd sheet of paper is about here. And my arm is tired from all this writing. Be good and continue to help out as much as you can. If you do everything pleasantly, that alone helps a whole lot. Everyone enjoys seeing a smile. No one likes a frown, scowl, or sullen expression. I love you honey. Keep up your piano practice. I want some good music when I get home.

Loads of love to all.
Azever with love,
Daddy

* * *

Postmark: February 8, 1961

Tues. 7 Feb 61
Almost wrote July!

Dear ones:

I forgot to tell you that my military history professor is a colored major. He is a brilliant man—has taught the same subject in several ROTC college programs. Most important of all, he is an educator instead of an instructor. We are required to do considerable more work than would be the case under a regular college professor, but he isn't as bad as the other officer teachers I had at the Pentagon and in Seoul (I dropped the class before I began when I learned how much extra work would be involved). Also, our class in history is very informal. The guy in Seoul did everything by rank and, as you know, that doesn't give me much of a chance.

My darned stove has been going out sometime during the night. Fortunately, the weather isn't too cold right now and maybe I can get the heater man to clean up the carbrunetor before I do any real suffering. But it's cold enough so that I wake up when the heater fails. Consequently, for the past couple of mornings (around 3 a.m.), I have been up trying to get a fire going. Last night the darned thing went out twice! So I get it fixed today, for sure.

Have decided upon what I'd like to do with my "living room," I am going to get rid of all furniture, clean up the rug, put up curtains & make up a cover for the bed (keep it for Campbell or some guy from 6th that may need to bed down once in a while) and buy one pearl inlay table (about size of coffee table) for the center of the floor. I'll put up pictures and a curtain between the 2 rooms.

And that's it. Col. Audet has his living room fixed up with both Japanese style & American style furnishings. But he has a big room. I am going to fix mine up American style Japanese, if that is clear—fewer items needed that way and what I get I can bring home with me.

I received a note from the maid today. I'm enclosing it to show you results of Americans being in Korea for 10 years. He is telling me she needs money, in case you can't tell. Who doesn't? I was about to hit her up for a loan. She's almost the only one I've missed. Col Audet is in Japan 8-20 Feb and she will be paid for one man (me) which will reduce her income considerably, as well as cost me more—we both lose on the deal.

111

The summer weather disappeared this afternoon with arrival of wind. I got the heater fixed (I hope) and should be comfortable tonight. Surely enjoy my room more now. I got a jar of instant coffee and a box of ginger snaps so that I can get my 10 p.m. snack before going to bed. I now have room to pace. I didn't realize how such a small room was affecting me. The one I had measures 10 x 14 and had a heater (3 x 3 on metal tray), desk & chair, occasional table, upholstered chair, night stand, dresser and bed. The extra room adjoining gives me a 10 x 14 space with only a bed at one end of the room. You can see that it does make a considerable difference.

It surely is nice to be able to shave all my face with an electric razor. I feel so much cleaner that I wonder how I put up with a moustache for almost 20 years—more than that, I wonder why you let me suffer so long. Until I get some more trimming on my hair cut, the less said about it, the better. But the way it stands right now, I look like a new man. Better or worse is a matter of opinion.

Battle of hi-fi going on again tonight—one at a time wouldn't be bad (I usually enjoy the record selection) but 2 at a time aren't good when I hear one about as well as the other. I can't do much fighting with my National 9/AFN combination. News casts aren't good for fighting music under any conditions—impossible with equipment distribution as it is.

I think that I have just about completed my ESC form 52's. A WB employee (18 yrs. service) is checking it over now. When he completes his review, I will go to CPO and get someone there to check it for me. When you get it, all questions should be answered satisfactorily. It looks to me like the only job I can apply for is one with CIC or OSI and it would be hard to find an opening in a particular area. But you check it out when you receive the forms 52. It would be good to have some words of encouragement before I submit retirement papers but guess that wouldn't be practical. I'll have results of my physical back by the end of this month so that I can submit my papers around 1 March. We couldn't complete checking the CSC forms, get them to you, have you check on a job, and get word back to me by then. So we can just say, "it would be nice if we could know before applying for retirement."

Weather prediction for tomorrow = low 20 high 30. It was 39° this morning and 44° this afternoon. If the wind stays with us it is going to be uncomfortable outside. I have caught a slight cold, I think. Don't feel bad but need Kleenex occasionally. Guess the last couple of mornings of running around in my shorts, trying to fire up the stove, has left its mark.

Gotta stop and study, cleanup, too. Time passes. I still don't count days but the weeks are becoming fewer when I'll be on my way home. Unless things get worse, I think I can hang onto my marbles until then. Sometimes I wonder if it isn't already too late, though!

Loads of love to all.

Don't forget to get the battery checked occasionally. Oil should be checked everytime you add gasoline. The motor, brake cylinder should be checked whenever the car is greased (every 1000 miles).

Bye now.

Azever with love,
Hal

Chapter Six

Retirement

Before Hal knew it, he had received the approval of his retirement request and was on his way home to the States to Wilda and their four children in Fontana, California.

"Daddy, daddy," the children squealed with delight when they saw their daddy Hal walking up the walk to the home where he had never lived. (https://www.youtube.com/watch?v=b9VsIZF-xv8) (https://www.youtube.com/watch?v=aTrHjrf_-N0).

It was good to be back with his family, although it was a bumpy adjustment for everyone. With two teenaged daughters, a preteen son, and a ten-year-old son, his life quickly twirled from structured order to raucous confusion.

My Lord, what happened to these great kids while I've been gone, he wondered. He immediately did his best to take control of the situation, and with his strict discipline turned chaos into order.

Although his career with the army was over at only forty-four years old, Hal wasn't ready to actually retire completely, and his search for a new career began immediately when he arrived. Wilda had been watching the employment ads in the local newspaper and had saved a few for him. Most were either manual labor jobs or clerical, neither of which interested him, but when he saw the ad for automobile insurance adjustor with State

Farm, he was intrigued and called the contact phone number right away to learn more.

The position required both investigative skills and an intimate knowledge of automobiles, and he had both, as well as the requisite college degree that he had earned through University of Maryland self-study courses before leaving the Army. In fact, the job was perfect for him.

Hal picked up an application at the local State Farm office; it was a strange feeling, applying for a job for the first time in over two decades. After he interviewed with the company two weeks later, he was convinced that this was the career for him. One thing, however, gave him pause: He would have to leave his family again for two weeks of training at the corporate office in Bloomington, Illinois.

"Honey, we have survived being apart for a whole year," Wilda encouraged as they discussed it at the kitchen table that night. "I'm sure we can survive another couple weeks."

Initially, Hal handled bodily injury cases, where he sometimes interviewed horribly injured people to determine reasonable insurance settlements based on the facts of the cases. His tales of the effects of body meeting steel left strong impressions on his children as future drivers, and he ensured that they drove defensively—every other driver on the road was an idiot to avoid.

Because of what he learned in his new role, plus an incident that had occurred several years earlier when Carol fell out of the passenger-side door when Wilda had rounded a corner, he became convinced that seatbelts were imperative for his family's safety. It wasn't until 1968 that a federal law required that all new automobiles be fitted with seatbelts; however, Hal made sure that their cars had seatbelts long before then.

Hal's second career lasted another two decades, until he retired for good in 1978. This time, he enjoyed his leisure time, learning to fly an ultralight aircraft and building a replica classic car in his garage when he was more than seventy years old.

He and Wilda lived comfortably empty-nested in Santa Maria, California, travelling together back and forth across the country every year in their RV, until Hal died suddenly in 1999 at the age of eighty-two.

Chapter Seven

Memories of Hal

Not all of Hal's escapades made it onto the pages of a letter, and, although I encouraged him to write them down, unfortunately that never happened. Everyone who ever knew Hal remembers at least one incident that makes them chuckle.

There was something about Hal—his sister, Doris, called him a "Kidder-bug"—but he liked to say or do the unexpected, the outrageous.

There was the time that he was visiting the home of a coworker and, unbeknownst to the parents, facetiously told the couple's young child, "Why don't you go outside and steal hubcaps."

The boy left and came back a short time later. "I couldn't get the hubcaps off, so I took the gas cap," the little boy reported, offering the proof in his tiny outstretched hand.

There are some stories that I recall but many more that I don't. Perhaps someday someone should collect the stories of family members and friends and put them on paper for you to read. If you have a story to share, contact me on Facebook. (https:// www.facebook.com/search/top/?q=carol%20e.%20yorke)

Review Requested:

If you loved this book, would you please provide a review at Amazon.com?

CPSIA information can be obtained
at www.ICGtesting.com
Printed in the USA
LVHW020401140420
653368LV00002B/385